SYSTEMATIC ADVISOR MARKETING

HOW FINANCIAL ADVISORS CAN STRATEGICALLY ATTRACT, CONVERT, & RETAIN MORE CLIENTS

Systematic Advisor Marketing: How Financial Advisors Can Strategically Attract, Convert, & Retain More Clients

Advisor Press c/o The Prepared Group

811 SW 6th Avenue #1000

Portland, OR 97204

advisorinbound.com

thepreparedgroup.com

ISBN: 9798607002480

Printed in the United States of America

A SPECIAL BONUS TRAINING FOR ALL READERS

How To Win More Clients Through Systematic Relationship Management

Visit **advisorinbound.com/clients** for FREE access

In this presentation, you'll discover . . .

- The proven follow-up system for converting more leads and prospects into clients based on a study of 3.5 million leads across nearly 400 companies.

- Exactly what type of follow-up is needed and when to deploy it.

- An automation platform you can use to be well on your way to follow-up superstardom faster than you can say "let's meet for coffee!"

Table of Contents

Introduction

"Hi, is this Mr. Baer?"

The voice on the other end of the phone almost sounded as if she was apologizing in advance for what she was about to say next.

"My name is Sarah. I'm a recent Oberlin graduate, and I was wondering if you had a few minutes to talk."

"Of course," I said. "I'm always glad to help out a fellow Obie!"

And with that, she launched into a script about her new job at a nationally known insurance company, and how she needed to "practice" meeting with prospective clients and showing them some of her insurance offerings.

Assuming I was simply being asked to help her out, we agreed on a day and time for Sarah to come by my office to "practice."

What I didn't know until the day arrived, was that while Sarah was there to *practice*, her boss, Rick, was there to *close* a sale.

Aggressively.

The entire experience left a terrible taste in my mouth, feeling like I'd been bullied into buying a product I didn't want or - at the age of 26 - have any idea I even needed.

To make matters worse, Sarah soon decided financial services wasn't for her and my account was moved to someone new to the business. While the new guy, Jake, seemed nice enough, I viewed him as just another salesman whose job it was to suggest ways for me to part with my money.

So, I ignored Jake's calls and spent the next decade avoiding anyone who worked in the insurance or financial services industry.

If only things had started out differently when I was first contacted by Sarah, I would have gotten an earlier start on my financial planning. That's because the most successful financial advisors earn their clients based on *trust*, and keep their clients based on relationships.

But I'm getting ahead of myself. Before we share our method for building the advisory business you've been dreaming of, I need to share how we got here.

Ken (my partner at Advisor Inbound and co-author of this book) and I have both worked as traditional marketers, each running our own agencies in the past, and working with a variety of clients in many different industries.

Clients have hired each of us for a variety of reasons. To build or improve their website, to write and design sales materials, to create and manage online ads, and a ton of other "marketing" activities.

When you think about it, what they were really hiring us to do was bring them more customers. Customers who would spend more money with them, so their businesses would realize bigger revenues, so the owners of those businesses could take those profits and spend them on things that were personally important to them... like a new house, or a family vacation or college tuition for their kids.

But I'm about to tell you something counterintuitive. More traffic, more leads, or even more customers doesn't always mean more profits. Ken and I both learned this the hard way.

For instance, Ken and his team once worked with a pest control company that was getting leads from online ads. When Ken took over the ad campaign, his client was spending around $250-300 in advertising to sign up a new customer.

Not only was Ken able to drop that cost-per-acquisition down to $42, but he was also able to drive more customers to the company than they'd ever seen before.

But there was a problem.

The pest control company didn't have the capacity to take on all the additional work Ken and his team were sending their way. Since they were unable to keep up with the demand, their work became sloppy, clients were leaving as quickly as new ones were coming, and money was being spent that didn't grow revenue for the business.

When examined through the lens of the modern marketing world, the marketing campaign was doing its job, or so Ken thought. But if his client's business was suffering, clearly there was a problem. That problem took Ken down the path of data-driven marketing, focusing on analytics, process and ultimately looking at marketing as responsible for growing company revenues not simply running "good" campaigns with "good" vanity metrics.

I also had my share of clients with problems.

Most went something like this: "I need help with Facebook ads, David."

"Sure, what are you trying to promote?" I'd ask.

They'd typically reply with something along the lines of "I need more customers."

To which I'd ask, "Okay, what's your offer?"

"Offer? I don't have an offer. I just want them to come to my website."

One look at the websites these business owners wanted me to send people to from Facebook ads told me there was little chance they'd be seeing many new customers as a result of my efforts. The sites I saw were poorly positioned to make sales, let alone get visitors to take an action like requesting an appointment or signing up for an email list.

Marketing, you see, is not just about getting prospects to show up. It's about...

- Making your ideal clients aware that you exist and what you can do for them.

- Helping them discover how your solution addresses the problems that concern them the most.

- Starting and maintaining a relationship until your prospects are ready to do business with you.

- Investing further in your most valuable asset (your existing clients) so you can build on those relationships and earn additional business from them as a result.

To put it another way, *everything is marketing*. Every interaction you, your staff, or your brand has with a client is marketing.

Which is exactly why Ken and I moved away from the typical "lead generation" marketing model we had previously worked under toward a holistic, systematic marketing approach - the exact system you're about to discover for yourself.

The Advisor Inbound Method

"There are literally thousands of ways to find business prospects to really build your book of business. Prospects are everywhere and this means on billboards, trucks, on the television, on the radio, on the internet, in newspapers, in networking groups. They're everywhere. All it takes is the ability to act on these leads and to make it happen by making that first introductory telephone call." - **Mr. Cold Call**

I don't know about you, but I've never been comfortable in the traditional "sales" role, which has made it challenging for me to hunt down and close prospects.

And I'm not alone in my discomfort with selling.

Most advisors I've spoken with tell me that their early days in the business were spent cold calling, an activity none of them have told me they enjoyed. After all, it takes a great deal of emotional strength and commitment to know that 19 out of 20 times you pick up that phone, rejection is waiting on the other end.

While cold calling might be a rite of passage for many new advisors, it also plays a key role in the high churn rate for those early in their career. Advisors who manage to stick around after "doing time" cold calling are quick to jump to less stressful business-building tactics as soon as they can afford to do so.

To be certain, the effectiveness of cold calling is entirely dependent on the list of prospects you're reaching out to. Working your way through the phone book (as some advisors have told us they've done) is probably going to be much less effective than working through a list of your firm's past prospects who previously demonstrated interest in financial services and simply need to be re-engaged.

But to assume that anyone and everyone is a prospect - and it's "just a numbers game" (as plenty of sales professionals believe) - is at best inefficient and at worst ineffective.

There is, of course, a better way: letting your ideal prospects come to you.

In the marketing world this approach is known as *inbound* marketing. It places the burden of the first move on your prospect as opposed to you. Cold calling, by contrast, is an *outbound* marketing activity that requires you make the first move by reaching out to prospects. The biggest downside to *outbound* marketing is that prospects are not expecting to hear from you and may or may not have any interest in what you are offering.

Conversely, prospects from an *inbound* campaign self-identify as having an interest in your offer (or, at the very least, they recognize a potential need for your expertise) and are volunteering to receive more information from you.

Using an *inbound* versus *outbound* approach to your marketing will make a dramatic difference in bringing you a great many more qualified prospects who will require less education and convincing than if you'd first connected with them through a cold call or networking event.

> *What a man believes upon grossly insufficient evidence is an index to his desires — desires of which he himself is often unconscious. If a man is offered a fact which goes against his instincts, he will scrutinize it closely, and unless the evidence is overwhelming, he will refuse to believe it. If, on the other hand, he is offered something which affords a reason for acting in accordance with his instincts, he will accept it even on the slenderest evidence.* **– Bertrand Russell**

The basic choice to employ *inbound* over *outbound* tactics is certainly appealing to advisors who want to simplify prospecting efforts. But the real success doesn't come merely from employing *inbound* marketing in lieu of other options.

The true advantage of an *inbound* approach is your ability to better manage your prospects and clients at every point in your relationship with them. Because when you start the relationship using a client-centric approach (it's all about them) as opposed to a sales-centric approach (it's all about you), your prospects and clients are much more willing participants.

This is precisely why we've developed the **Advisor Inbound Method**, our systematic approach to advisor marketing.

To be clear, we didn't invent this approach. Over our years of working with small and medium sized businesses, we've found gaps in their attempts to attract, convert, and retain customers. And as we've implemented solutions – some we already knew and others we discovered along the way – we cherry picked the most effective elements, which we've compiled into our method, and we are sharing with you here.

The Advisor Inbound Method is broken down into eight clearly defined steps, each of which we'll cover in greater detail over the next several chapters. But let's start with a quick overview now.

In any advisor-client relationship, there are three general categories:

1. The pre-engagement period

2. The initial engagement (when your clients first begin to work with you)

3. The service delivery period

Within each of these three categories, there are specific activities you, as the marketer of your practice, can choose to take control of.

During the pre-engagement period...

- **Attracting Prospects.** The most effective way to attract prospects is to identify a narrowly defined target group who have a problem they need solved and insert yourself or your practice in front of them, offering a solution.

- **Capturing Their Information.** Offering your prospects an opportunity to preview your solution (without committing to becoming a client or even having to speak with you) provides you with a means of collecting their contact information. Giving access to a brief guide, or video, or webinar or even a live seminar can provide a value-based, frictionless way of collecting their contact information for future use.

- **Nurturing The Relationship.** Not everyone interested in learning about your solution is likely to become your new client right away. In fact, most won't. By establishing a routine of regular and consistent follow-up, you can continue to build a relationship with prospects until the point they are ready to move forward.

At the point of initial engagement...

- **Converting Them Into A Client.** In order to make the right offer to prospective clients at the right time, it's important to understand their decision-making process and establish a system to manage the conversation designed to set you up for a sale.

- **Making It Easy To Get Started.** Often overlooked or taken for granted, sometimes a new client can get stalled before they've even gotten started because the process is intimidating and confusing. But when you plan ahead so you can assist new clients in getting started, you're more likely to keep them moving forward.

During the service delivery period...

- **Delivering A "Wow" Experience**. Far too many advisors lose clients because after the initial sale, the tone and frequency of communication changes dramatically. Instead, when you create a process of delighting and "wowing" your clients, you'll not only retain them, you'll benefit from additional opportunities to extend the services you provide them, as well as earn more referrals from them.

- **Furthering The Relationship.** Stemming from the work you and your team do to delight and "wow" your clients, you'll earn the right to offer them additional products and broaden the range of services they'll consider investing in with you.

- **Getting Referrals.** Most advisors believe their business is referral-based. And yet, few advisors have a true system for getting referred. When you've done the necessary advance work with your clients and circle of influence, asking for and receiving referrals can be a snap.

These are the eight basic steps that comprise the Advisor Inbound Method of building a thriving practice.

So, What Makes You So Special?

There's a lot of competition out there trying to get the attention of consumers. Commercial banks. Discount brokerages. Insurance brands. Robo-advisors. Newsletters for DIY Investors. And hundreds of thousands of captive and independent advisors going by all sorts of titles from "Registered Representative" to "Investment Advisor" to "Financial Planner" to "Chartered Financial Consultant" ...and the list goes on.

With so many people and entities out there, how are you expected to compete? How can you get people to consider you and your services over all else? The answer lies in something known as a Unique Selling Proposition (USP).

Your USP answers this vitally important marketing question, first posed by marketing consultant Dan Kennedy:

"Why should I, your prospect, choose to do business with you versus any and every other option, including doing nothing?"

Businesses often use their USP as the headline on their website or a tag line on their ads, so consumers know exactly what the company's place is in the market.

Having a powerful USP makes it easier for prospects to choose you, and it helps you attract the *right* clients to your practice. It also helps you avoid attracting the types of clients with whom you don't want to work. But if you don't have a USP, or if you have a weak USP, it will be hard for prospects to differentiate you from everything else out there. By default, most will see you simply as a commodity provider, competing based on price.

A well devised USP needs to be a true reflection of what your clients experience when working with your practice. That means it can't be a meaningless tag line that's all style and no substance. For example, imagine dining at a restaurant that promotes itself for elegance and haute cuisine. When you arrive, you find a giant screen television over the bar tuned to ESPN, burgers and pizza on the menu, and a wine list that looks like it's been written by the restaurant's beer distributor. Your experience doesn't match the USP they've used to attract your business.

Could you imagine shopping at Target one day and finding their prices to be on par with Neiman Marcus, Nordstrom, or Saks Fifth Avenue? Or how would you feel if you walked into the Nordstrom shoe department and received the service and quality that you would normally find at Wal-Mart?

In our minds, we have a very clear idea of each of these retailers' places In the market and know what to expect from them before we ever enter their stores. They each have different Unique Selling Propositions. Wal-Mart promotes itself as a price leader, while Nordstrom is all about quality and service. And yet, both of them make money and satisfy a partition of market demand. Each has its own USP and attracts customers accordingly.

Most financial advisors don't take advantage of this simple - yet critical - step in establishing their practice. But when you do take the time to determine your USP you'll be at an advantage, better able to grow and survive in today's marketplace, and beyond. It starts with being able to successfully answer these two questions:

1. Why do people work with you?

2. If they aren't working with you now, why should they?

What you're after here is some kind of a sustainable competitive advantage. Something that sets you apart from your competition or makes you unique. Of course, "unique" is a loaded word. And with so much competition out there, the likelihood is you're not the only one doing what you do and thinking it's unique.

That's why you need to establish a Unique Selling Proposition that your competition doesn't offer, creating extra value or giving people additional reasons to work with you. Unique Selling Proposition can take form in at least four different ways.

It can:

Be the price leader. This means that out of all the competitors in the market, you offer the lowest price. This is a great advantage if it can be created and maintained. However, it's often difficult to consistently be the price leader and, unless you're a giant discount broker with millions to spend on advertising to the masses, this probably isn't the right USP for you. Many companies make the mistake of trying to be the price leader, working on tiny margins and aiming for high volume sales, which often causes them to go out of business. If you have the means to compete as the price leader, great. If not, you shouldn't play that game.

Differentiate. This means that your practice can create an advantage by doing something more or better or different than the competition. It could be in the form of longer hours, better guarantee, higher quality, more selection, better service, etc.

Focus on a certain niche. This means that your practice can zero in on only one small segment of the market and then become either the price leader or differentiate in some other way, but only to that small segment of the market. We'll be going into detail on this approach in the next chapter.

Extra Value Proposition. Your practice provides more value, more quality, more service than your competitors.

Without an effective USP, people will never know why they should consider your services. And, in the absence of any other perceived value, the buying decision on the part of the consumer will always be price. As we already established, being a price leader probably isn't right for independent advisors.

So, in order to help you frame a USP for your practice, here are some important characteristics of effective Unique Selling Propositions:

1. Be able to articulate the proposition in 90 words or less. Answer the question: Why should people do business with you and not your competitors?

2. Quantify the benefit as much as possible.

3. Be specific in the areas of quality, service, selection, guarantee, etc. A USP is not a mission statement.

4. Fill a void the competition is not filling.

5. It must matter to prospects and clients.

6. It evolves based on what competition does.

7. You must be able to execute the proposition.

Determining Your Unique Selling Proposition

Domino's Pizza is famous in the marketing world for identifying a void in the pizza industry and filling it. Their USP became "If we don't deliver your pizza within 30-minutes or less, it's free." Those exact words were communicated in all advertising whenever you saw an ad on TV or in print. It was clear to all people that Domino's had the fastest delivery and they guaranteed that if it didn't happen, your pizza would be free. They built their empire around this USP, and it worked. They didn't say "we make the best pizza" or "authentic pizza just like your Mamma used to make." Nope. Their USP was built around speed and a guarantee. If you're hungry, we'll feed you FAST!

The Men's Wearhouse has built a tremendous business strictly on price. Back in the early days of the company, the owner, George Zimmer, would appear on TV ads emphasizing over and over, "Remember, no one – I repeat, no one buys clothes at a lower price than at The Men's Wearhouse – I guarantee it!" And while Zimmer was ousted from the company after 40 years at its helm, the price USP still remains. People go to The Men's Wearhouse clearly understanding that the price is better there than at any other clothing store in the area.

Nordstrom has done a superb job in distinguishing their *higher end clothes* from competition. They have emphasized this strongly and their salespeople are clearly trained in the concept. If you are unhappy with your clothes, bring them back for a prompt exchange or refund. They also have a personal shopper program. You can call up the store and a personal shopper will gather your clothing options for you. You meet them at a certain time and choose from the clothes they have picked for you, saving you time and effort.

Each of these companies has recognized a void in the marketplace that they've successfully filled. Now it's your chance to determine (or, if you don't already have one, decide on) your Unique Selling Proposition. You'll start with a survey of both external and internal factors, and once you've analyzed your results, you can extract your USP.

This survey was something that Ken created to help our team quickly understand new clients as they came through the door. It allowed our team to have real clarity on what made a practice unique, and in an industry where so many people sound the same it created real clarity around each business' strengths and weaknesses.

Here are the survey steps:

1. Do you compete locally, regionally, or nationally?

2. How many others are in the financial services field in the geographic area where you are competing? This would include any individual or

institution in the broad category of financial services, including banks, accountants, brokers, advisors, etc.

3. How many others are directly competing in the sub-category of financial services in the geographic area where you are competing? This would include any individuals or institutions providing a similar set of offerings to those you offer.

4. How many others are in the single category of business you focus on (retirement planning, investing, tax planning, etc.) in the geographic area where you are competing?

5. List 3-5 advantages you have over your competition in your answer to question #4.

6. List 3-5 disadvantages you have compared to your competition in your answer to question #4.

7. Describe the competitive landscape (Here we're looking at not simply other businesses, but also the general economic, social factors that are part of your reality.)

Finally, when you take all of these facts, views, opinions into account you come to this as a conclusion:

8. What are the beliefs the market has around the service you provide?

If you're scratching your head, struggling to figure out how to answer these questions, here's a quick look at how we filled out the survey for our business, and the USP we created as a result:

1. Do you compete locally, regionally, or nationally?

Nationally

2. How many others are in the marketing field in the geographic area where you are competing?

There are hundreds-of-thousands to millions of marketing consultants, marketing agencies, and marketing freelancers.

3. How many others are directly competing in the sub-category of marketing in the geographic area where you are competing?

There are several hundred thousand marketing consultants working with small-to-mid-sized businesses in the United States.

4. How many others are in the single category of business you focus on in the geographic area where you are competing?

Fewer than 250 marketing agencies or consultants competing to work only with financial advisors

5. List 3-5 advantages you have over your competition in your answer to question #4.

We're a small, nimble, agile team, allowing us to devote optimal time on each client project.

We have a broad range of experience to inform how we execute our work (which means we're not delivering cookie-cutter solutions).

We don't limit our services to online marketing, giving our clients additional guidance and support in areas like seminar marketing and direct mail.

We are constantly investing in our own education to enhance the value we deliver in each and every client project we take on.

6. List 3-5 disadvantages you have compared to your competition in your answer to question #4.

We're small, so we limit our new clientele each month.

Clients can't just "set it and forget it" when they work with us. They need to actively participate and be willing to change course as data dictates.

Working with our team isn't within reach of every advisor's budget.

7. Describe the competitive landscape

Advisors have a great many options when it comes to marketing their practice. They can do it themselves, buy into a compliance-approved vendor program, hire an independent marketing firm, and so on. Each solution offers a different set of services, usually differing in quality and price as well. Not all solutions fit every advisor's priorities, but most advisors don't know their full scope of options (nor have they fully considered their priorities), so education is typically required before sales of marketing services are made. Therefore, there is limited understand of the benefits of a "systematic" approach to marketing.

8. What are the beliefs the market has around the service you provide?

Most marketers are in it for a quick buck. They send advisors unvetted, unqualified leads who aren't ready to buy, and money flies out the window without any clear ROI.

Our resulting Unique Selling Proposition:

"At Advisor Inbound we help advisors attract, convert, and retain more clients through customized lead generation and client nurturing programs."

Now, it's your turn.

Practical Implementation

What Makes You So Special?

1. Do you compete locally, regionally, or nationally?

2. How many others are in the marketing field in the geographic area where you are competing?

3. How many others are directly competing in the sub-category of marketing in the geographic area where you are competing?

4. How many others are in the single category of business you focus on in the geographic area where you are competing?

5. List 3-5 advantages you have over your competition in your answer to question #4.

6. List 3-5 disadvantages you have compared to your competition in your answer to question #4.

7. Describe the competitive landscape.

8. What are the beliefs the market has around the service you provide?

Attracting The Right Prospects

"Platitudes and generalities roll off the human understanding like water from a duck. Actual figures are not generally discounted. Specific facts, when stated, have their full weight and effect." - **Claude Hopkins**

True story.

I used to attend a monthly networking event called "Network Before Work" here in Portland, Oregon. There were typically sixty to eighty people in attendance. Among the usual suspects, there were always 8-10 financial advisors.

The room was set up like an enormous conference room and we were all seated around the perimeter of the room facing each other. One by one, we were given sixty seconds to introduce ourselves and pitch our services.

One month it seemed like every advisor in the metro area decided to show up for "Network Before Work" because, one after another, I kept hearing the same basic introduction and pitch:

"Hi, I'm Joe Advisor, and I provide financial planning services for anyone who wants to secure their family's future, be prepared for unexpected expenses, and retire in comfort. I take a holistic approach in my financial planning and investing strategy. If you or anyone you know can use my services, please see me. Again, my name is Joe Advisor."

Typically, our group would hear a pitch like that two or three times through the meeting. They were usually followed by someone who had an interesting story about how their bakery had just appeared on Food Network or how they were a Olympic kickboxing champion and were opening a new studio. With stories like those, the advisors were quickly forgotten.

But on the day in question, I counted seven advisors sitting along the same side of the room (with only one non-advisor sitting between them). One following another, they stood up and recited the same basic generic introduction. I'm not sure if it was my lack of coffee or the uninspired presentation from these advisors, but I nearly nodded off to sleep.

Until the final advisor in the lineup.

Instead of repeating the same timeworn introduction, this guy recognized the irony of the situation.

"Hi, I'm probably the eighteenth financial advisor you've heard from so far this morning, and I don't expect I'll be the last. I won't bother telling you my name, because you'll probably forget it. The reason there are so many of us here today is because as a profession, we recognize that so many people struggle to put their limited financial resources to good use, so we help people make decisions to be able to better afford the life they desire. If you've got questions about financial planning or retirement or protecting your assets, I sincerely hope you'll take advantage of the opportunity to speak with one of us while you're here today. Oh, and if you'd like to find out my name, please see me afterward."

There were a lot of advisors in attendance that day, but at the end of the event, none had a line of people waiting to speak with them... except this guy.

Why?

Because he stood out.

He didn't really say anything different from the other advisors. However, he did slightly change the perspective of what he was saying.

When he got to the part about how advisors see "so many people struggle to put their limited financial resources to good use," and how they help people "better afford the life they desire" he succeeded in getting the attention of a handful of people.

For the people who lined up to speak with Joe Advisor #18, he said something that resonated with them. The lesson here, as the great writer of the early 20th century, Robert Collier, put it, "Always enter the conversation already taking place in the customer's mind."

What Collier meant was that you need to present your service or your offer in the context of what your prospects are thinking about at a particular moment in their lives. Another way to approach this concept is to consider what's keeping them up at night.

For the advisors at "Network Before Work" who used words like "secure you family's future," or "be prepared for unexpected expenses," or "retire in comfort," they missed an opportunity to connect with what was on their prospects' minds.

But when Joe Advisor #18 used the words "put your limited financial resources to good use" a few people in the room probably thought to themselves... "Hey, I've been trying to figure out how to use the little money I have more effectively. Maybe I should talk to this guy."

In case you're wondering "how am I supposed to know what's going on in my prospect's mind," here a simple (and extremely effective) way to figure it out:

Get Super-Specific About To Whom You Are Marketing Your Services

The more narrowly you are able to define your ideal client, the more effectively you can identify and speak to the things which matter to them most.

Sure, you *can* serve "everybody," but imagine how much time and money it would take to promote your services to all those people and get a tiny fraction of them to say, "out of 300,000 financial advisors, you're the one for me!" If that's your plan, we hope you've got really deep pockets and years to develop your brand... because the only other types of businesses who see any benefit from marketing to "everyone" are companies like Ford Motors, Coca-Cola, and Apple.

That's why when we say "super-specific," we mean it.

"Business owners" is generic. "Owners of closely held family businesses" is super-specific. By narrowing your focus to "family business" owners, you can speak to them in a more meaningful way about both their desires (like creating an income legacy for their family) and fears (like creating an exit strategy or transitioning ownership to the next generation).

Here's another example of a super-specific prospect. Instead of "parents," which is too generic, how about creating messaging for "first time parents" and offering them a guide to smart family financial planning?

Or, if you're targeting solo practitioners of veterinary medicine, you might use messaging around practice transition, tax tips for veterinary practice owners, or financial services based on what point they're at in their career.

By selecting a clearly defined, super-specific audience to target, you're giving yourself an entry point into presenting your solution. One that's going to matter more to them than a staid, tired, generic offer.

This approach is commonly known as "niche" or "target" marketing. If you're new to this concept (or you've simply been avoiding it), here's how it works. There are several different ways you can target your marketing.

The first approach is to present yourself as a specialist in solving a specific problem. For example, many advisors position themselves as "retirement rollover" specialists. But you could just as easily specialize in inheritance investment or college financial planning.

Another approach is to target individuals based on an affinity or personal connection. For example, working with members of your house of worship or aligning yourself with a professional organization or your local chamber of commerce can be highly effective. We know advisors who promote themselves to alumni of the college they attended as well as advisors who promote themselves through their sorority or fraternity.

By creating and packaging a special offer to people who identify with a particular community, you're borrowing that community's authority or stature in the minds of those you're targeting.

Finally, there's the most common approach we see to target marketing. That's self-identification. Like the examples we shared above, first time parents, owner of closely held family business, and solo practitioners of veterinary medicine. This is an approach that requires you to use marketing messaging related to the way people see themselves. Again, don't be too broad or your message won't resonate.

Targeting "doctors" might seem specific enough, but doctors who are in residency and dealing with repaying medical school debt have a different set of concerns than a cosmetic surgeon in Boca Raton who's been twice divorced and has three kids in college. You can't easily speak to them both with the same marketing message.

3 Reasons You Should Choose a Target Market

If you're still resistant to the idea of target marketing, not to worry. As we dive deeper into the Advisor Inbound Method, you'll discover how to leverage your decision into clear and calculated activities.

Marketing to a specific audience not only helps you create and use more effective marketing messages, but also gives you direction when it comes to where your prospecting time and money is best spent.

Here are three benefits of target marketing that we'll be exploring further in later chapters:

1. Your marketing prospects, clients, and referral partners will better understand exactly what you do and precisely who you serve, because your marketing messaging is so dialed in and finely articulated.

2. Prospects who fit your ideal client profile will be more likely to want to work with you over a generic "jack of all trades" advisor.

3. Clients and professional partners will find it easier to refer you based on your specialty in serving a specific audience or expertise in providing a particular service.

You'll be able to better determine where to invest your marketing efforts. When you know who you're targeting, you'll also be able to determine where they hang out - and be most likely to encounter your marketing message. Consider what organizations or associations they might belong to, what publications they read, and what websites they might visit. Showing up in a place where your prospects are (and where your competition isn't) will give you a distinct advantage to starting conversations.

Pretty much any target market has some sort of established network or means of communication. It might be a mom's group that meets in the park every week or an association newsletter (where you can advertise or contribute articles). Targeting a super-specific audience will open up all kinds of opportunities to leverage existing connection and communication channels.

How To Talk To Your Target Market

The key to success in communicating with your target market is to speak to them in the language they use. And that means you avoid "financial services" jargon as much as you possibly can.

For example, let's say you're discussing taking "required minimum distributions." Do you think your target market understands what you're talking about if you use those words? Probably not. Just like professionals in other industries, you've become comfortable with the language of financial services. But nine and seven eighths times out of ten, your prospects and clients are NOT!

So, what words might work better in this instance?

How about "the amount of money required by law to take out of your retirement account each year after a you reach a certain age?"

The meaning of common industry terms might seem obvious to you. But, when you step back from your everyday conversations and consider what words you're using, you'll probably realize that you're using words that make it harder for your prospects to connect with you. In these instances, they tend to stop paying attention, and start trying to figure out what the heck you just said. And when that happens, you've lost momentum, and have probably already lost a sale or two.

Practical Implementation

Identifying Your Target Market

As an Advisor, you have big dreams. You want to build a practice that brings you satisfaction and success. You want to talk to the right people so that you can serve them, making their futures more secure, even as you secure your own.

While the concept of an ideal client may be nothing new to you, we want to clearly state that "pre-retirement, with at least 500k in investable assets" is not a target market. This is like when you hear realtors tell you they are looking for buyers OR sellers, it's like a doctor saying they are looking for sick people. It's true but it's radically incomplete and it's a recipe for failure in marketing your practice.

We also know that it can be easy to spend huge sums of money trying to attract the wealthy pre-retiree to your services, only to find that you've overspent your budgets and you don't have any new clients. It's hard to get noticed in this clutter filled world but attempting to reach "everybody" who could use your service is not only inefficient, it's also very expensive. That's why it's important to narrowly define your target client and meet them where they are. The following exercise is designed to give you a complete picture of your ideal client, which you can leverage as you work to attract and convert them.

Who are my ideal clients? (Use demographics such as age, annual income, and education level. Use psychographic information such as behaviors, hobbies and values.)

Example:

My ideal client is a man, 62 years old who has become a widower in the last two years and now feels lost as to what to do with his retirement because his focus for the last 30 years has been taking care of his wife. He attends church occasionally, enjoys sports, especially baseball and loves to watch games in-person. He values family and relationships and has worked in a middle management role in a Fortune 500 company for the majority of his career. He also values transparency and communication above bargains.

What are their pain points?

(Efficiency, ease of use, time, etc.)

Why should they buy from me? Why should they choose me over my competitor?

What are their most common objections to doing business with me? (Cost, time etc.)

Who is NOT my target client?

Building Your Target Client Avatar

An *avatar* is a tool often used by marketers to identify a representative individual of your ideal client. It helps bring humanity to the masses you speak to. It allows you to have a person in mind to ask yourself about likes and dislikes. This will drastically improve your overall performance because it will allow you to focus more effectively on your target audience.

As you consider the following characteristics, consider both *demographics* (the average or typical characteristics of your target market) as well as the *psychographics* (what motivates them to take action).

Age: When looking at age, David and I typically encourage you to give no more than a 3-5 year age range. This really allows you to narrow down to whom you are speaking.

Gender: Men and Women respond to different tones, messages, and offers. They care about different things and picking to whom you are speaking will direct you to speak to those concerns.

Marital Status: Married, Divorced, Single, Widowed…

Children: How many and what age(s)?

Income: We would push you to limit your income range to no more than a 5k range.

Education: What level of education and where did they receive it?

Personal Beliefs: What Religious or political beliefs are held, and to what degree are they valued?

Hobbies: What does your prospect do for fun? What do they wish they could do more often?

Values: What are your prospect's deeply held values? Do they care about Money, Family, Community, or the Environment?

Location: Where are you most likely to encounter your target market?

It's All About... Them

*"It is not from the benevolence of the butcher, the brewer, or the baker that we expect our dinner, but from their regard to their own interest." - **Adam Smith***

First, some bad news.

The vast majority of your prospects don't care about you.

This may sound like a liability, but, it's not. Because, when you follow the system we're outlining in this book, you'll be positioned to attract and serve more clients than you'll know how to handle.

The key to your success is understanding these two things:

1. Your prospects' interest in you and your services is directly related to the fact that you can either help them solve a problem or help them achieve a desired goal. In other words, they are primarily focused on themselves - and will be far more responsive to your marketing efforts if you focus on *them* as well.

2. The decision to work with you will be overwhelmingly based on emotion (though it will likely be justified by logic). Study after study has shown that humans make decisions based on feelings, not facts. If your marketing is built entirely around facts and figures, and lacks emotion,

you're missing huge opportunities to connect with more prospects.

With that in mind, how do you use your prospects' self-interest and emotional decision making to your advantage?

Offer Your Prospects Something They Will Value

There are two general approaches to marketing: *brand marketing* and *direct-response marketing*. Brand marketing is all about getting your name widely known and recognized. In general, you'll see category-leading companies invest heavily in this type of marketing. The goal with this approach is to connect the business or product name with their category in the consumer's mind.

While brand marketing is used by the big wire houses, banks, and other financial institutions, it requires an enormous capital investment, and return on investment is very hard to track. Those are just two reasons why financial advisors should not waste time or money on brand marketing.

Direct-response marketing, on the other hand, allows businesses to present offers directly to consumers, getting them to take a specific action. Examples of direct-response marketing might include

TV or radio ads promoting a toll-free number for people to call to order a free cosmetics kit sample, request a life insurance quote, or join a class action

lawsuit. Or it could be an online form offering a free guide about weight loss or dating or investing guide.

These type of "special offers" are known as lead magnets and are usually provided free or at a nominal cost to the consumer in exchange for their contact information.

Why do businesses collect contact information?

One reason, of course, is to be able to deliver the promised gift (the lead magnet). Another reason is to be able to follow-up with the consumer to make additional offers, extend invitations, or sell something. Your prospect and customer data is a resource that holds tremendous value and in the future will only appreciate in value.

For advisors with a target market, there's no need to use generic lead magnets like "10 Things You Should Consider When Hiring A Financial Advisor" or "Pre-Retirement Checklist."

Instead, you can consider your prospects' self-interest and emotional decision making to create a lead magnet that's meaningful to them.

For example:

- "The Divorced Woman's Guide To Financial Independence"

- "The Five-Day Family Financial Plan"

- "Are You Making These Financial Mistakes in Your Dental Practice?"

- "Wealth Preservation Guide For Family Business Owners"

While lead magnets are often delivered as a PDF or as email content, they can also take the form of web content, a video, a webinar, a live seminar, or even a phone consultation.

We often like to think of lead magnets as long-form ads or sales letters in disguise. Because, essentially, their job is to sell the next step in the relationship between you and your prospect.

There are lots of components to a well-structured lead magnet. For some guidance on the subject, let's get...

Advice from A Fighter Plane Wing Manufacturer

It may sound like an unlikely source for getting lead magnet advice, but Max Sackheim actually ran one of the last century's most successful direct mail businesses. Prior to starting his agency in 1945, he was a co-founder of the Book-of-the-Month Club and later ran a company which made... you guessed it... fighter-plane wings in World War II.

He wrote several books on advertising, all of which are long out of print. However, if you look hard enough, you can occasionally, find used copies online for a few hundred dollars. Even though Sackheim is long gone, his observations are still highly relevant today - and 100% applicable to producing great lead magnets.

We'll save you the trouble of hunting down his work, and summarize the key points of his book, "Seven Deadly Advertising Mistakes: Conclusions Based Upon 45 Years of Experience with Keyed Advertising." These seven points are something that we use on a very regular basis and have been shown to been timeless gems that will supercharge your lead magnets. So, without farther ado here are the seven deadly mistakes that sabotage your lead magnets:

Mistake #1 - Failing to Give The Reader a Reason to Read Your Ad

Your prospects won't care about your content if they don't know where you're leading them once they start consuming it. Therefore, you need to make a promise to them up front, so they'll stick in there with you to receive the promised pay-off at the end.

Mistake #2 - Using Headlines That "Whisper Sweet Nothings"

Headlines are powerful (the *original* Mad Man, David Ogilvy, often said that "On the average, five times as many people read the headline as read the body copy. When you have written your headline, you have spent eighty cents out of your dollar.") Make sure your headline packs a punch emotionally and is meaningful to your prospects.

For emotion, two of the most effective types of headlines are *fear-based* and *curiosity-based*.

And when it comes to connecting with your prospects in a headline, try calling them out by their self-identity ("The Single Mom's Guide To...").

Mistake # 3 - Using Pictures That Do Not Talk

You've heard the saying that a picture is worth a thousand words, right? Using images in your content can reinforce emotion or literally "illustrate" a point you're making. The right images can also make your content more memorable.

Conversely, images that seem to have no connection to the content, lack emotion, or are obvious stock photos, can sometimes detract for your content's main goal (getting your prospects to move forward in your sales process).

Mistake #4 - Giving In To The Curse of Cleverness

There's no problem being informal or even a little humorous in your content. But if you come across as trying too hard to entertain (this often happens on webinars and live presentations when presenters have an unnaturally high amount of energy) it can turn prospects off.

Remember, you're selling yourself. To set the right tone, it's best to gauge your ideal clients' expectations, and find the right balance between being staid and boring, and too lighthearted.

Mistake #5 - Going Around Robin Hood's Barn

Here, Sackheim is talking about staying out of the weeds. The less you make your prospects jump through mental hoops to understand what you're telling them, the more effective your lead magnet will be.

One of the best lessons we ever learned about copywriting and business communications was to talk and write at a fourth-grade level. As someone once said (it might have been Mark Twain, but we can't find evidence anywhere), "you'll never offend a sophisticated man with simple language, but you'll surely offend a simple man with sophisticated language."

Mistake #6 - Leavin' 'em Dangling

Lead magnets are the beginning of a relationship. Once your prospects have finished consuming the content, tell them what's next. Make sure to include what's referred to as a "call-to-action."

We'll often use lead magnets to show people how to accomplish something. At the end of the content, they'll have learned the "what" but not the "how."

So, we'll say something like... "You've just learned the 6 critical steps to creating a high converting home page for your website. If you'd like to truly master the art of getting more of your website visitors on your appointment calendar, request a strategy session with Ken today!"

Mistake #7 - Using "Yackety-Yack" Copy

Don't waste your prospects' time. While we encourage storytelling (something we'll discuss later) to help support the points you make, it's important to avoid "fluff" in your content. Make everything you say interesting, useful, intriguing, or curiosity-provoking.

Practical Implementation

Attract More Clients To Your Practice

Once you know who your target prospects are, you'll need to find out where they're most likely to come in contact with your practice and be receptive to your messaging.

Think about location both online and in person. Are they on a particular social media platform? Do they attend local business events? Are they members of a local community or work in the neighborhood?

After you've identified where your prospects are, we recommend that you focus your efforts. Perhaps this means that you need to join a local networking group or chamber of commerce, volunteer with a civic organization, start a new social media account, or spend some money on targeted advertising.

Be where your prospects are and start engaging with them in an authentic, helpful and personable way. Use lead magnets like videos, free reports,or giveaways (like dinner seminars) to attract more of your target audience to your business.

The following questions will help you dive deeper into your targeting for your ideal clients:

Where do my clients "hang out?"
(Social media, online, conferences, etc.)

What would attract them to my services?
(Educational materials, reports, etc.)

What lead magnets are currently working in my practice?

New lead magnet ideas:

(Videos, investment trends, etc.)

Lead Magnet Brainstorm

What are some common mistakes that you help people avoid?

What are the underlying goals your clients have?

Examples:

- *3 mistakes most people make when [Investing in their IRA]*

- *Do you make these 3 mistakes in [planning for your long-term care]?*

- *3 common [investing] mistakes you don't know you're making*

- *3 tips for successfully [retiring in] your [50's]*

- *3 things you absolutely need to know about [index funds]*

- *3 proven techniques to [secure your retirement]*

- *3 new tricks to [maximize your income in retirement]*

- *3 keys to fixing your [income] problem*

What are the frustrations people have when they buy from your competitors?

Examples:

- *3 questions to ask your [financial advisor] before you hire him*

- *3 mistakes rookie [advisors] make when [selecting annuities]*

-

- *3 things to consider when [choosing your Investment Advisor]*

- *The 3 biggest problems with [picking stocks]*

What are your clients curious about or trying to learn?

- *3 Questions I always get asked about [investing]*

- *3 things they should have taught in [college] about [investing]*

- *3 Tips for dealing with [a bull market]*

Four Types of Lead Magnet

Identify your lead magnet gaps and categorize them below.

Important / Urgent:
(I need this type of lead magnet yesterday.)

Important / Not Urgent:
(I already have this lead magnet and it's working.)

Unimportant / Urgent:

(I already have this magnet but it's not working. I need to trash it.)

Unimportant / Not Urgent:

(I don't need this lead magnet.)

Collecting Your Visitors' Information For Follow-Up

As you begin attracting more clients to your business, you'll want to make sure they don't leave and forget about you. Now that you've attracted the right audience, you need to either make the sale or get their contact information so you can follow up with the leads that aren't ready to buy just yet. You can capture leads by providing them with something of value in exchange for their contact information, like a free trial or sample of your product or service.

Build trust and give your prospects a reason to opt-in. E-books, podcasts, videos, webinars and downloads are just a few content assets that you can offer to build trust with your audience and establish credibility for your brand. Make it easy to opt-in with the right lead capture tools, like a web form on your blog or website.

How many prospects am I attracting and how many leads am I collecting each month using the following?

Website:

Events:

Blog:

Direct Mail:

Telephone:

Networking:

Social Media:

PPC:

SEO/SEM:

Walk-in:

How can I capture their information?

Discussion board:

Networking event:

Have employees ask:

Demo Drawing/Contest:

Online Form:

Badge scanner at an event:

Lead Generation Card (on social media):

Other lead capture methods:

What can I use to organize potential clients once I have their information?
(Database, spreadsheets, CRM, etc.)

Where are your lead collection gaps?

Let's Do The Numbers

It's Ken here. David's handed over the reins to me to discuss a topic most advisors - most businesses, in fact - overlook. That's their numbers.

having been in the marketing industry for about a decade at the time, but on my own for only about 4 years, I had a client for whom we had built a pretty predictable system - we knew that for every $63.37 we spent on marketing, we were signing a new client! That was a heck of a deal, as the minimum this person was signing for was a yearlong contract, for no less than $600.

This client, when he first came to me, bragged that he changed marketing companies every 3-4 months. It was like a badge of honor, or maybe a warning -- who knows... But as I dug into the marketing that this growing company was engaging in, I found that no one was measuring anything! And I mean NOTHING... So, I sat down with the owner and asked him how much money he would be happy spending on a new customer.

He said $5.

I smiled and laughed -- in awkward anticipation of a more realistic number... but none came.

I then asked how much he'd be able to profitably spend on a new customer.

He said he would typically, on his base sale, spend about $450 all in on operations and service. He then revealed that at "no point" had any marketing group been able to allow him to make money on his first year with a client - something that I took as a challenge...

So how did I get him to be profitable in the first six months of a new client relationship rather than in the first eighteen?

It was Peter Drucker, the father of modern business leadership, who taught "what gets measured gets improved." There is real truth to this idea, especially when it comes to marketing, and the rise of data-driven marketing has led to a near frenzy over measurement and analytics to understand how to improve marketing.

I believe that if we're to be successful in growing businesses we must have a firm grasp on the numbers. However, metrics are in and of themselves, not the salvation we are looking for in the marketing world. They are simply a tool.

"In the end, there is no silver bullet, no substitute for actually knowing one's subject and one's organization, which is partly a matter of experience and partly a matter of unquantifiable skill. Many matters of importance are too subject to judgement and interpretation to be solved by standardized metrics. Ultimately, the issue is not one of metrics versus

judgment, but metrics informing judgment, which includes knowing how much weight to give to metrics, recognizing their characteristic distortions, and appreciating what can't be measured. In recent decades too many politicians, business leaders, policymakers, and academic officials have lost sight of that." — **Jerry Z. Muller**, The Tyranny of Metrics

John Wanamaker famously commented that half of his marketing was wasted, though he didn't know which half. Many have tried to remedy this commonly healed belief that marketing is simply trial and error. Some have attempted to create predictive technology, others have invested in supposedly better targeting, and still others have advocated for changing or adding new marketing channels.

The truth, however, is there is no silver bullet to predicting marketing outcomes without the essential ingredient of data from previous results. All other efforts are simply a waste of time and money. And yet, most advisors are in the dark when it comes to how much they are wasting when it comes to marketing. Are you currently calculating your ROI? What about your acquisition cost?

Data is the key. Because when you use data to inform the metrics you'll use as the basis for your marketing decisions, you're going to drive more effective growth in your practice.

How?

The single focus of metrics is the elimination of waste. Measuring what you put in and what you take back out of your marketing allows you to effectively eliminate the things that don't drive the bottom line:

getting new, retainable, clients. Everything we do in measurement is in service to this goal.

So, with this end in mind I'm going to layout three different marketing measurement frameworks for your consideration. I'll do my best to avoid getting too deep in the weeds here, but this is a subject that deserves some deeper understanding among business owners like you.

The first framework is basic funnel measurement. It is a step-by-step accounting of where people are in your sales process, and it will allow you to see exactly what kind of prospecting / marketing actions lead to specific results.

The second framework that I am going to explain in this chapter is a more advanced variation of the first that will allow us to better understand what kind of prospecting / marketing activities lead to specific revenue outcomes and will give us some level of future predictive power, in that regard.

Finally, the third framework is going to dig deep into your practice. It's going to answer questions like, how profitable is my practice? -- what is my time worth? -- how can I scale my practice?

The "secret" to your success here is knowing your numbers and using them to make smart choices.

Framework 1: Sales Activity & Client Retention At-A-Glance

Let's assume you follow a sales process in which you have two appointments to close a new client. Sometimes it's more, sometimes it's less. But you average two appointments. Typically, a first appointment might include a general exploration of the prospect's needs and your services. A second appointment, sometimes known as a discovery appointment (but we've heard lots of other names used), provides an opportunity to present a specific plan and seal the deal with your new client.

In an effort to track your sales activity toward conversions, we recommend compiling data on each of the following items on a weekly, monthly, quarterly, and annual basis:

New Cold Prospects. People with whom you have little to no relationship, but you have at least one of the three critical pieces of contact information and permission to contact them (ie. Phone number, email, and/or mailing address). Ideally, there would be some qualifications in place to filter these new prospects so that you don't simply have a large "list" of prospects who can never be qualified into warm prospects.

Warm Prospects. People with whom you have some relationship, and have met some qualifying criteria.

First Time Appointments. People who have actually had a first meeting with you.

First Time Appointments Cancelled. Why keep track of this? Simple. It provides a predictive matrix showing you a ratio of "scheduled" to "kept" appointments. This is critical so you can base your actual performance in these meetings, and isolate cancellations from unqualified prospects (such as lack of personal fit, disconnect with your investing method, or lack of personal means).

Discovery Appointments. The second meeting held with prospects that are on track toward becoming a client.

Signed Clients. Like Alec Baldwin said in *Glengarry Glen Ross*, these are the folks once you "get them to sign on the line which is dotted!"

Retained Clients. This is a little bit of a less intuitive metric that I often see is missed, because it's nothing more than your current client count. However, this can tell you about the size of your front door versus the size of your backdoor. (According to a

Financial Advisor Magazine article from May of 2019, as many as 45% of clients leave their advisor in the first two years of the relationship. 20% of those leave in the first year!)

Referrals. I know that you live by referrals but let's not be a ship tossed about in the sea about them. Let's get a real grip on what's happening on this front. Ideally, these are the referrals that are 1) meaningful, and 2) meet enough criteria to get the person into warm prospect status!

The reason to track all this data is not to sit back and bask in the knowledge of your numbers but rather, it is so that you can employ a methodology for improvement of each of these metrics. This is where Excel becomes your best friend. Simply keep track of each of these items from week to week. This doesn't need to be complicated, but it does need to be accurate.

Framework 2: Financial and Channel Driven Metrics

Framework 1 should give you a good overview of what's happening in your business, which is useful for at-a-glance updates. But it's only useful if you're only using one marketing channel or means of attracting prospects.

Therefore, the focus of this second framework is to apply financial metrics to the process and separate your prospects by channel. We know very few established practices that use only one means of attracting prospects, so if you're only using the data of the framework 1, you're missing out on insights

 into how each marketing channel is performing. The following metrics will remedy that:

New Cold Prospects by Channel (Metric: Action Cost). For these we are looking at the channel, the number, AND the cost to acquire what typically amounts to an opt-in request of some kind (i.e. a white paper download, information about a seminar, signing up to watch a webinar, etc...). For example, if you spent $500 on Facebook ads and you received opt-ins to a web presentation on retirement, you have a cost-per-action of $50.

Or if you spent $1500 sponsoring a chamber of commerce club for a year and you got one new lead each month, we could say that you have a cost-per-action of $125 ($1500/12 = $125).

Warm Prospects (Metric: Unqualified to Qualified Ratio). For this framework we're looking at a ratio of cold to warm prospects, again by channel. So, if on Facebook you take 50% of your cold prospects and they become warm prospects, you could say that you've moved from ten cold prospects to five warm prospects.

First Time Appointments (Metric: Lead to Appointment Ratio). For this you're creating a financial metric using your cold prospect numbers and your ratio of cold to warm prospects. This is going to tell you what it actually costs for a booked appointment. So, if it requires 5 warm prospects to

book an appointment (and we know that based upon our Facebook example above) we can book one appointment.

Signed Clients (Metric: Acquisition Cost). This is where perhaps the most valuable marketing metric comes in. We now have all of the data in place for us to be able to drive to a final acquisition cost (measured by channel, that is). If we know that for every 3 first time appointments we sign one client, we know that our acquisition cost is $1500.

Retained Clients (Metric: Average Customer Value). This is where you get to measure the average value of your clients gained by specific channels. We're going to look at customer value generated by each channel. Now, I know that this is likely NOT a weekly metric, but it is ideally something that you can look at on a quarterly basis.

The best way that I've found to calculate this is to make it an aggregate average, meaning if you have $30 million of AUM for 25 clients produced from Facebook, you can get a pretty clear picture of what an expected average new client from that specific channel is worth. You can also take multiple channels and bring those averages together to get what your average client is worth.

Referrals. This may feel a bit like beating a dead horse, but simply asking for referrals is insufficient for measuring the actual outcome of these referrals. We can't tell you the number of practices we've seen that "work primarily off referrals" who have no idea of the numbers behind those referrals! That's why we recommend tracking referrals just like you would any other channel and getting each of the above metrics for this channel and comparing it to each of your others.

This framework, which primarily deals with the financial metrics of client acquisition, is useful for two main purposes. First, it allows you to see what activities are profitable and in what timeframes they will become profitable. Second, it gives you financial predictive power, that when applied to Framework 1 gives you a clear guide for what kind of money your efforts will bring you.

A word of caution about this framework. The biggest pitfall for this is poor tracking. If you can't tell which channel generated the lead, the entire system breaks down. We dislike relying on client surveys for this information and would strongly recommend that you put in place a systematic process for identifying and cataloging who came from a specific channel.

There are a number of great Client Relationship Management (CRM) tools that can help you accomplish the outcomes metrics described above.

Framework 3: Scaling Your Practice

This third and final framework of the Advisor Inbound Method really focuses in on longer term values. What this means is that we're going to have a few metrics that we look at on a quarterly and annual basis that tell us about the overall direction that the business is going.

Net Income Per Hour of Operation. This might sound like quite the mouthful, but the concept behind it is very simple. How much profit do you make per hour of operation? The best way to really get to this number is to start with your net (after tax) revenue for the quarter and divide it by 520 (this is assuming a forty-hour work week for thirteen weeks). So, if your net after tax was $10k in Q1, your net income per hour would be $19.23. This is often a shocking metric, because it's often hard to have business profitability in mind during the day-to-day activities. The goal for this metric is to drive operational thinking.

Churn Rate. There's nothing fun about calculating the rate at which clients will leave you, but that is what your churn rate is going to tell you - and it's an important metric to track. We know a number of advisors who take and start building "wow" into the practice (which we'll be covering in detail later) and have seen their churn rate dramatically reduced.

How to calculate churn: Take the number of clients that you lost in a given timeframe (quarter or annual is typically what David and I use) and divide that by the number of clients that you started with in that same timeframe This will give you a percentage or a churn rate. Let's say, for example, you started the quarter with 125 clients and lost 8 of them in that quarter. You're going to have a quarterly churn of 6.4%.

Growth Rate. You're probably very familiar with this metric. You likely use it to evaluate stocks regularly, but have you taken this inverse of churn rate and applied it to your business? If you have, would you invest in your organization based upon it? I'm not saying that you need to apply compound annual growth rate (CAGR) to your business, but having a simplified picture is going to tell you how your organization is performing.

How to calculate growth rate: This is going to be a calculation similar to that of churn rate. Take the number of total clients at the end of a timeframe and divide it by the number of total clients at the beginning of that timeframe.

So, if you begin the quarter with 125 clients and you ended with 145, you would have a growth rate of 16%. Where this starts to become a powerful tool is when used in conjunction with churn rate.

Lead Velocity. This metric is about how many leads are generated within a given channel. Why does it matter? Lead velocity is something that you look at to tell you about the overall production potential of a given marketing channel. If you knew that the Chamber of Commerce's annual sponsorship gave you great results in terms of acquisition cost, but it only generated ten leads a year, this tells you about the scaling potential that this channel brings. It also speaks to the opportunity cost. If you have to spend money in January and wait until October to see a return, that may or may not be a great fit for what you're trying to accomplish.

Are there other metrics that we could consider?

Absolutely!

The field of analytics and the selection of key performance indicators (KPIs) is vast, and we have not even begun to scratch the surface of this critically important topic.

My aim here, however, is not to give a masterclass in metrics, but rather to give you the metrics that are the most effective in global measuring of the effectiveness of your marketing.

These are the numbers that we use on a regular basis to understand how well our clients' practices are performing and growing. We know that

for many advisors the implementation of these may seem overwhelming, but our hope is that you'll start simple, and realize that consistency in measurement is the key.

Remember, there is NO silver bullet.

The Other Nine

"The three most important words in marketing are follow-up, follow-up, follow-up. It ain't gettin' 'em. It's keepin' 'em." - **Jay Abraham**

Let's imagine you're running ads each month to drive prospective clients to make appointments with you. On top of your ads, you spend time networking and hosting a monthly lunch and learn with small business owners.

You've got a budget of $1,000 per month to spend on ads, and you're dedicating about 10 hours each month to prospecting activities. These may not be the right numbers for your practice, but we're using round numbers for this example because they're easy to follow.

In an average month, the money and time you've invested brings 100 prospects your way who express interest in accessing your lead magnet or learning more about how you can help them.

And out of those 100 people, you're able to schedule appointments with 10 percent of them, ultimately converting one of those 10 people you meet with into a client.

That means, for every $1,000 spent and 10 hours per month invested, you're adding one new client to

your business. Put another way, your "cost-per-acquisition" for each new client is $1,000.

Now the average advisor will look at this math and say to themselves, "If I want two new clients each month, all I need to do is double my investment." In other words, spending $2,000 each month and 20 hours on prospecting activities.

But we're assuming you don't want to be the *average* advisor (that's why you've invested your time to read this book, right?).

You see, most advisors are actually wasting time and money in their prospecting and marketing activities. In fact, there are three major areas where we see waste taking place:

1. Wasted Traffic. This might include website visitors, people who respond to your ads, people referred by their friends, and even those who register for and attend your seminars. Many of these people have a limited amount of interest in working with an advisor NOW, so they're unmotivated to move forward with you.

When it comes to website visitors, most advisors have no idea who has visited their site. Maybe the advisor is smart enough to prominently display their phone number or include a contact form on the site so people can get in touch (though you'd be shocked how uncommon even something that basic tends to be). Even less common is a clear call-to-action (CTA) telling the site visitor what to do to start a relationship (or even an inquiry) with the advisor.

The Solution: As we discussed in *It's All About… Them*, you must capture your lead's contact information.

2. Wasted Sales. When it comes to an in-person meeting, as we discussed in the scenario above, only one of ten prospects will become a client right away.

So, what happens with the other nine?

Well, the *average* advisor, who finds that a prospect isn't going to hire them right away, usually squanders the opportunity to control what happens next. At the end of the meeting, they'll thank the prospect for making time to talk, hand them a business card, and ask them to get in touch if and when they are ready to move forward.

Perhaps the advisor is savvy enough to follow-up with the prospect. But the average number of follow-ups is between 1 and 3. And yet, according to compounded studies across hundreds of sales organizations in the United States, Canada, and Britain, 80% of non-routine sales occur only after at least <u>five</u> follow-ups.

Think about that. It takes at least five follow-up efforts after the initial sales contact, before a prospect says yes.

- 44% of sales people give up after one "no."

- 22% give up after two "no's."

- 14% give up after three "no's."

- 12% give up after four "no's."

That tells you that 92% of salespeople give up after four "no's," and only 8% of salespeople reach out a fifth time.

When you consider that 80% of prospects say "no" four times before they say "yes", this means that 8% of salespeople are getting 80% of the sales.

The Solution: In case you've not been paying attention, you must follow-up 5 or more times to close the majority of those other nine who weren't ready when you first met.

Wasted Clients. Your existing clients are a huge marketing asset to your practice. Unfortunately, most advisor overlook them. As a result, clients may choose to leave from time to time. Industry surveys have shown that the biggest reason clients leave their advisor is the result of poor or complete lack of communications. And, when they do communicate, it's often bad news. In fact, according to a BNY Mellon / Pershing study, 58% of advisors only reach out when markets are down and 68% only reach out when the client's personal investments are down. Imagine having your clients only associate you with bad news.

The Solution: Better communication, of course. As well as a few additional ideas we'll be sharing with you when we discuss *delight and "wow."*

Your Follow-Up System

Want to know the number one reason advisors don't follow-up with unconverted prospects more than a couple of times? Because they think it takes too much time.

But when you think about that $1,000 and 10 hours invested, wouldn't you rather lower that $1,000 cost-per-acquisition? Think about it. If you did enough follow-up to close just one additional client each month, your cost-per-acquisition would be cut in half. And if you were able to eventually close 8 out of the original 10 after enough follow-up, your cost-per-acquisition would be $125 per new client.

Wouldn't that be worth the extra time? We'd argue that it would be... even if you did all of the follow-up manually. But nobody's suggesting you do it manually. There are plenty of client relationship management platforms and lots of marketing software that can help you automate the entire follow-up process.

For example, we create custom follow-up systems for advisors we work with, designed to send out emails on a regular basis, as well as prompt the advisor or someone else in their office to reach out by phone at certain intervals.

A good follow-up system isn't just about "checking in" with prospects, of course. Email and phone outreach can (and should) continue to add value to the relationship you've started with a prospect.

Just as you did with your lead magnet (discussed in the previous chapter), be sure to make your outreach content interesting, useful, intriguing, or curiosity-provoking. Most of all, ensure that it's relevant to your prospect's interests - which is so much easier when you're working with a specific target audience.

The best follow-up content to send them builds on the subject of the lead magnet they initially requested from you. That means if you shared information on retirement planning for public employees, you want to continue sharing content that would relate to their status as a public employee.

You may be tempted to demonstrate your expertise as a financial professional by sending them market updates or industry reports, but that would be a mistake for two reasons:

1. Most of your prospects won't find this sort of information relevant to the reason they originally connected with you.

2. It's more about *you* than it is about *them*.

Every time you communicate with a prospect, be sure to consider how the communication is relevant to them, and what you want them to do after hearing from you. And always, always, always include a call-to-action.

Practical Implementation

Education as a Sales Tool

Consumers will only pay attention to you when they're motivated to do so, and the best way to gain their attention is through interaction and education.

It's important to understand your prospects before you can create content that's relevant to them. As you build out your content strategy (blog posts, videos, email content, etc.), consider how your message serves your prospect's basic psychological or self-fulfillment needs. Then, build foundational content on your website, blog, social networks, or other communication platforms that address those needs.

We are big fans of the "They Ask, You Answer" methodology of content. What this means is that you provide true transparency and anticipate the questions your potential clients have. While entire books could be (and have been) written on this subject, we want to work to keep it simple. The most important thing is to keep your avatar in mind and answer in a way that would be moving to them.

The following questions will drive you to educate your prospects in order to sell:

What questions do potential clients have before they buy from me?
(Specific details, cost, process, social proof, etc.)

How can I address those concerns?
(Email series, white paper, website, videos.)

Where can I address those concerns?
(Blog, social media, newsletters, etc.)

Once I address these questions, what is the next logical step for a client to make?

(Request a meeting, attend an event, request or provide specific information.)

Converting Prospects to Clients

Prospect.

Qualify.

Present.

Close.

These are the four steps for making sales in just about any industry you can think of. Let's look at some examples:

- A furniture retailer might advertise to attract prospects to their store. After determining what the prospect is looking for, a salesperson presents options and asks for the sale. A further qualifying factor might come if the purchase needs to be financed.

- Attorneys might prospect by networking, or, if they practice personal injury or DUI law, they might advertise to find prospects. Next, they determine if the prospect is a candidate to work with them (often, a prospect might self-qualify themselves simply through the act of contacting the attorney). The presentation usually will involve a description of how the attorney works on behalf of their clients and may even present a specific strategy for the prospect's case. Finally, the attorney closes the sale by asking if the prospect wants to move forward.

-

- Pest control companies might prospect by using door hangers or cold calling businesses. They'll qualify by getting prospects to admit to having a problem that needs to be solved. A representative of the service provider will be dispatched to inspect the property, present a service offer, and ask for the sale.

- And, of course, financial service professionals' prospect through a host of different methods (cold calling, email outreach, LinkedIn, direct mail, advertising, networking, etc.), qualify prospects based on things like investable assets or ability to pay fees, present service options and ask for the sale.

While these four steps *should* happen in each and every sales scenario, the sad truth is they usually don't. One common problem we see with advisor businesses all the time is that they don't do a very good job qualifying their leads until they are trying to close the sale. Another problem we see a lot is ineffective prospecting activities.

Imagine how much better the sales conversions for these advisors would be if they were prospecting for the right people, using the most effective methods to reach their target audience and making certain to qualify prospects before offering a presentation. It's simple math. And yet, most advisors don't take the time to consider where their best sales opportunities are coming from.

Let's assume you're running ads on Facebook to a free offer for a PDF download. This campaign is bringing you a 42% opt-in rate to your prospect email list and you're converting 1.7% of those who join your list into clients, with an average revenue of $2,500 per sale. Unfortunately, at the rate of advertising and cost of follow-up, you're actually losing money on this initial sale.

So, where is the problem?

It's actually a trick question, because the answer could lie in multiple places.

For example, are you attracting qualified people to the free offer, or are you getting a bunch of freebie seekers who would never consider hiring you?

How much follow-up is involved in moving a prospect from your email list to a meaningful conversation that would set them up for a presentation from you?

Is your presentation structured effectively so that it connects with your prospect's stated wants and desires? Have you pre-empted their objections by addressing them before they even get raised? Have you included enough material to influence their emotional decision-making process?

If you're not asking these questions about your selling process, it's a sure bet that you're missing out on more conversions.

The Sales Conversation

It doesn't matter if you call it a "financial assessment," a "discovery session," a "free consultation," or something else. At some point you'll be sitting down with your prospects to have a conversation where you'll be making an offer to work with them.

In other words, the "sales" conversation.

Now if you've taken the time to attract a super-specific targeted prospect, and you've used a lead magnet that's been designed to speak directly to them, addressing a problem they know they have... you'll be well positioned for a successful sales conversation.

This is, in part, because you've communicated with the emotional part of their mind in a way that makes rational sense to them. Those who self-qualify as candidates for your services will want to move forward with a sales conversation. Those who don't identify with your process or solution will self-select out, either by ignoring your communications or simply unsubscribing from your emails. Don't be upset or offended. They were probably never going to become a client anyway.

So now that you've got (hopefully) qualified prospects in a conversation to discuss your services, it's time to turn the conversation to cold hard fact-based discussion of their finances and the various financial vehicles you might use to help them get where they want to go... right?

Not on your life!

You've worked hard to get them to this point. Now, more than ever, is the time when you double down on what brought them to this point... focusing on the problem or aspiration that brought them to you in the first place.

That is accomplished by following a process.

Now, we're not sales coaches (we're marketing strategists, and sales involves a somewhat different set of psychological triggers), and we're not here to advocate one selling system over another. So, go ahead and use SPIN selling, The Sandler System, The Challenger Sales Method or Same Side Selling or anything else that you'd like. But make certain that, no matter what approach you take, you are sure to include a) plenty of stories to help illustrate the opportunities you're presenting, and b) a clearly articulated offer.

What's an "offer," you ask?

Put simply, an offer isn't the specific product or service you are selling. Rather, it's a way of presenting what you are selling so that your prospect can fully understand the benefits of each feature and is more likely to say "yes" than they are to say "no."

There's on old saying when it comes to writing sales copy: mediocre copy and a good offer will out-pull great copy and a mediocre offer any day of the week.

Having an offer in place allows you to structure a sales conversation that connects your prospects pain points and desires to the various benefits of your solution. It's also a useful mechanism to use when it's time to ask for the sale.

That's important, because no matter how good at "closing" most sales professionals believe they are, it's universally believed that somewhere between 80% and 90% of them never actually ask for the sale (losing out on a ton of money as a result). But that's a subject for a different book.

Let's return to the subject of making an "offer."

You've probably seen variations of it in long form sales letters you've received in the mail or multi-page text-based newspaper ads, or at seminars where a pitch is made following a presentation. In these instances, the presentation is not really a "conversation" because it's usually one sided. But you could certainly guide your sales conversation to cover the same ground.

Here's one way to consider structuring the sales conversation:

1. Start with some simple report building.

This is the usual banter "how was your weekend?" that mere mortal advisors will likely take for granted as exchanging pleasantries. But not you. No, you'll be sure to listen for information that's worthy of adding to your client database. This might include offhand comments about family members, special occasions being celebrated, yacht club memberships, ballroom dancing lessons, etc. (This kind of information about your clients can prove extremely useful in the future - stay tuned for more on this topic in a later chapter.)

2. Outline the agenda for the meeting.

This is your chance to set up the close by telling them an offer will be forthcoming later on in your conversation. But first, you'll be wanting to learn more about their challenges and goals so you can customize exactly what you'll be presenting later on.

3. Identify the problem(s), desire(s), and general facts.

This section of the meeting is often not given the amount of time and attention it deserves. That's a shame, because this is where the real meat exists in your ability to get your prospects to convert into clients. It's often described as identifying problems, extracting the real pain behind those problems, and then agitating that pain, asking what would happen if it's not addressed. This is where you need to be a good listener and an exceptional note taker, because these themes will come up again later on in your conversation... and, likely, later on in your relationship with this client.

This is also a good point to find out about existing assets and collect other details about the prospect's familiarity with the financial world. It also sets you up nicely to segue to...

4. Talk about money.

The topic of how you get paid and in what amount is, curiously, something many advisors try to avoid. This makes no sense. After all, you're a financial services professional, and talking about money is a central part of what you do for a living. Bringing up the topic at this point in the conversation helps qualify your prospects ability to pay (which may or may not be important depending on your business model) and gets the information out in the open so the curiosity of "how much will this cost us?" isn't distracting them from your conversation.

5. Find out how they make decisions.

Advisors often find themselves in the dark about why a prospect didn't come onboard. They're not certain if they should follow-up, and if so, how often or how much. By asking questions around this topic, it will help you know how best to manage your prospect through the decision-making process.

6. Use *future pacing* and storytelling to connect their desired outcome to your offer.

Future pacing is a technique used to help prospects consider what it would like to achieve the things they've told you they desire or problems they want to overcome. Earlier in the conversation, you gathered a lot of information from your prospect around concerns and wants they have, and hope will be addressed by working with you. This is the moment to revisit those topics and use stories to paint a picture of how working with you can help achieve their desired outcome.

Because you have so much information about them at this point, you can weave their story into your offer. For example, one way to present an "offer" is to outline your process, and, as you explain each step, insert how it will specifically benefit your prospect by using the information they've shared with you.

For example, let's assume they've told you that they have a certain risk tolerance, and at some point, in your conversation you discovered they are very interested in environmental issues and sustainability. You might say something like, "well, Mr. And Mrs. Jones, one of the first steps we'll take is to review your investment goals against criteria that best reflects the things most important to you. For example, I know one of your goals is to save for your daughter's college fund, and you also said something earlier that indicated we might want to consider looking at socially responsible investment options. This first step will help us pinpoint a plan just for you."

Now, even though a great many advisors would probably take these same actions as part of their onboarding process, the fact that you highlighted two items (their daughter's college expenses and environmental concerns) they've shared with you, can be a tremendously positive emotional trigger as they move toward making a decision to work with you.

7. Outline your offer by focusing on benefits.

If you've ever watched an infomercial or an ad for one of those "as seen on TV" products, you've probably encountered a selling technique known as "the stack." It's basically a piling on of bonus items you'll receive when you purchase the item they're promoting. For instance, not only will you get free shipping, but if you order right away, they'll also throw in a second item at no extra cost, plus they'll include a travel version and a free guide showing you all the ways you can use the fancy doohickey they're selling.

While you probably don't want to be so cliché as to utter the words "but wait, there's more," you can use a variation on the stack to pile on the value of what your prospects will receive when they decide to become a client. Again, while other advisors may include everything you do, they are probably not taking the time to highlight the individual components of their service, and most will certainly not take time to articulate the benefits either. Using your version of the stack will put you at a distinct advantage when it comes time to...

8. Ask for the sale.

While some advisors will "assume the sale" and move directly into the "getting started" phase, others will employ the Sandler approach of innocently

saying something like "so that's what I've got for you... what should we do next?" and await the client's positive (and hopefully obvious) reply that, duh, they're ready to move forward.

And then there's the simple, but direct, "so, would you like to join our community of clients?"

The point is, NOT asking for the sale at this point would seem far more awkward to your prospect than asking would.

So... Ask. For. The. Sale.

Practical Implementation

Make The Offer

In order to make the right offer at the right time, it's important to understand your prospect's buying process—the journey they go through before they decide to buy (or not buy) from you.

The best way to do this is to observe past clients' actions and create a buying process map. Then, match your sales process to their buying process.

If you have a sales team (or if you are the sales team) you'll want to optimize your resources so that you spend your limited time with prospects who are qualified. Lead scoring is tracking your prospects' behaviors and activities, so you can determine their varying levels of interest in your solution.

We have one client who uses this tactic and was able to increase his appointments, simply by targeting those who clicked on weekly emails. It's a great tactic to use that will help ensure that you spend your limited time on the people who are most likely to convert.

What is my compelling offer?

(What solution do I provide that addresses my prospects' pain points?)

When should I extend the offer?

(After they read the e-book, after a conference, when they initiate a call with an advisor, etc.)

What does my prospects' buying journey look like?

(How are buyers getting from "Do I have a need?" to a justified decision?)

How do I know when a prospect is "hot"?

What are some key objections that I will need to overcome?

What happens to everyone else who doesn't decide to become a client right away?

Close More Sales by ...

Closing the sale involves more than just an exchange of money or signed documents. In a direct sales conversation, the close involves clear communication, good presence, and written documentation. For advisors, the close is the signal that the deal has been negotiated and you can now begin the process of delivery.

Looking at your sales process the following questions will bring some illuminate the biggest challenge, making it easy for your prospects to become clients.

How do clients buy from me?

(Online, in person, sales team)

How do I make it easy to buy from me?

How can I make it even easier?

(What non-obvious items can we employ to make the process easier for clients to say yes)

What are the top 3 things I can do to improve my selling system?

1.

2.

3.

Is It Easy For Prospects to Become Clients?

*We see our customers as invited guests to a party, and we are the hosts. It's our job every day to make every important aspect of the customer experience a little bit better. – **Jeff Bezos, Founder of Amazon***

The best way to screw up a new client relationship is to make it hard to get started.

After all the careful work you've done to target a niche audience, learn and use their language to persuade them that you've got the answers to their super-specific problems, you've skillfully nurtured them into a series of sales conversations, and gotten them to say "yes," what do you do next?

Send them home with a huge pile of forms and a giant list of information you need them to compile, accounts needing to be transferred, and, maybe some instructions to access a private client portal on your website where they can watch some videos on uploading documents to their personal "vault."

After all of that, some advisors wonder why they don't hear from new clients for weeks or months on end after they've agreed to come onboard. Often the answer is that new clients are simply overwhelmed. And when faced with a seemingly large task or navigating unfamiliar territory, most people tend to procrastinate.

Before we can discuss the importance of client experience in-depth, it's imperative that you take a serious look at how you transition prospects into clients.

The reason for this is the initial interactions a new client has with you will set the tone for your entire relationship. The likelihood of a client sticking with you and recommending you to others increases with the level of prioritization you give to creating an excellent onboarding experience.

According to a Harvard Business Review study on B2B onboarding, "an increased focus on onboarding offers significant or moderate positive impact over the life of the contract for revenue, client renewals, and client referrals."

Looking at it from the other side, the costs of *not* having a successful onboarding process are significant, potentially causing problems such as...

- You are missing out on valuable feedback that could be used to improve your processes and services.

- Any trust you've built winning the client flies right out the window.

- Your closing rate for upselling or cross-selling additional services to existing clients can flatline.

- Unhappy clients write negative reviews or share their bad experience with others.

- If you depend on monthly recurring revenue, your client churn rate will go through the roof.

It's not just Harvard Business Review discussing this topic. In recent years, as consumers have easier access to information and a wider range of services available to them, traditional service providers like financial advisors must put client experience front and center if there's any interest in retaining your clients long term.

Develop A Client Onboarding Experience

When you consider how to onboard new clients, you can look at it in one of two ways: you can consider all the things your new client must do to get set up to work with you... or you can consider all the things your practice can do to assist your client in getting started.

These two approaches may not sound all that different from each other, but the amount of work you and your team do vs. the amount of work you ask of your client can be perceived vary differently by the client.

When your practice builds and implements a client-centered approach to client onboarding, one that's practiced by your entire team, client trust is stronger, client engagement is higher and the long-term bond between the client and the advisor is far greater.

You also set the stage for transforming a client relationship into a loyal client who will advocate for you and refer others your way because loyal, engaged clients understand the value you deliver for them, and are eager to introduce you to qualified prospects who can benefit from your products and services (more on this in the next few chapters).

Studies show that advisors who successfully onboard clients using a consistent, systematic process have a far higher client retention rate than advisors who ignore the importance of a client-centric onboarding process.

Of course, one size doesn't fit all situations when it comes to getting new clients started with you. Your practice and your clients will likely have a unique set of priorities that won't necessarily be the same for other practices or client types. While you might consider utilizing a "welcome" procedure that demonstrates the unique experience your practice provides, there are also some common onboarding activities you might consider.

For example...

- Creating a customized checklist for onboarding new clients. Include all of the details involved in bringing a new client into the practice, from all the paperwork that needs to be filled out to permission to communicate via email and on social platforms.

- Making sure that all team members understand their roles in onboarding a new client. Often, prospects who become clients have only met the advisor at this point. If other team members will be involved in servicing the client, find ways to incorporate introductions and educate clients about each team member's role in supporting them.

- Explaining the onboarding process to new clients. Not only will they benefit from clarity and certainty about the process, but you can also explain how the onboarding process helps you and your team better support them.

- Developing letters and email templates for your onboarding process. You don't need to reinvent the wheel each time you bring on a new client. Writing standard letters and email templates that can be re-used increases the efficiency of the client onboarding process and makes fewer demands on your staff, freeing them up to execute a higher level of client service.

- Maximizing efficiency and educating clients along the way. As you onboard clients, there's information that needs to be gathered and conversations that need to occur. When you set up meetings, make phone calls, send emails, and make other inquiries in a logical and predictable sequence, onboarding goals are accomplished and new client satisfaction increases.

- Distributing a new client welcome packet. A lot of the information you need to give to a new client, along with the forms they'll need to fill out can be gathered and placed in a branded folder and given to the client at the first meeting. This will increase efficiency and leave a good impression in the new clients' mind. (In the next chapter, we'll discuss other ways you can use your welcome packet.)

- Following-up with your team and clients to ensure tasks are accomplished. By creating a processes that your entire team is aware of, they'll know when and how often to follow-up with new clients to ensure that account transfers and other paperwork is signed and executed as quickly as possible, so you and your staff can start working on your client's financial and investment plan and implement that plan as soon as possible.

- Outlining a schedule for meetings, phone calls, and reviews. When onboarding new clients, let them know what the schedule is for the next few months. Schedule meetings and let them know when your office will be in touch and what type of communications to expect and when. For example, if you have a newsletter, include a copy of the most recent one and information on how often they can expect future newsletters and other communications, like phone calls and email updates.

- Surveying your new clients. No process is perfect, and there's always room for improvement. Plus, you don't know what you don't know. That why it's so important to survey new clients about your onboarding process to uncover any potential problems and to receive suggestions that could help improve onboarding in the future. Asking clients for their feedback can help them feel more connected to your practice and lets them know their views are being heard... all of which is important in nurturing a long term and successful client relationship.

Practical Implementation

Making It Easy

Creating a roadmap for you and your team to help onboard clients makes the process simpler for clients, which means a better overall client experience.

The following questions will help you in mapping out your onboarding process. If you already have a process the following will give you additional clarity.

The most important thing for our practice when a client is brought on is . . .

Do you currently have a master list of potential documents that clients could be required to submit and activities they must perform? How is/could this be communicated to the client? Who on your team is responsible for assisting the client with this process?

What are the steps a client must take during onboarding?

Who on our team is involved with a client during and after onboarding? To whom on our team does the client need to be introduced?

What is the biggest addition you can make to your onboarding process to make it easier for your new clients?

Delight and "Wow!"

Peter Shankman is a sought-after consultant and expert in how businesses communicate with their customers, a huge part of which is customer service. Back in 2011, he shared a story about an experience he had with Morton's Steakhouse. We love sharing this story in our marketing strategy workshops because it's probably the best example we've encountered of how to deliver an extraordinary customer experience.

Since it's Peter's story, he's agreed to let us share it with you here in his own words:

> *The following story is entirely true. More importantly, I swear on my entire professional reputation and all I hold dear to me that the story below was in no way staged, planned in advance, or in any way faked. This is real. And most importantly: This is AMAZING.*

> *When my alarm clock went off at 3:30 this morning, I knew I was in for a long day. I was catching a 7am flight out of Newark to Tampa, Florida, for a lunch meeting in Clearwater, then heading back to Newark on a 5pm flight, getting me in around 8:10pm, and with any luck, to my apartment by 9 or so. We all have days like that, they happen from time to time.*

Made my flight, everything was on time, got to my lunch meeting. Because of the training/workout schedule I'm on, my first meal of the day was that lunch. Was fine, I had a healthy piece of grouper, and a very successful lunch meeting that lasted just about three hours.

By the time I got back to the airport, it was close to 4pm. Flight boarded at 4:30pm, and I knew that by the time I got home, I wouldn't have time to stop for dinner anywhere, and certainly didn't want to grab fast food at either airport. When I got on the plane, my stomach was a rumbling a bit, and I had visions of a steak in my head.

As I've tweeted and mentioned countless times before, I'm a bit of a steak lover. I go out of my way to try steakhouses all around the world when I can, and it's one of the reasons, no doubt, that my trainer at my gym is kept in business. But it's all good – give and take. Over the past few years, I've developed an affinity for Morton's Steakhouses, and if I'm doing business in a city which has one, I'll try to schedule a dinner there if I can. I'm a frequent diner, and Morton's knows it. They have a spectacular Customer Relations Management system in place, as well as a spectacular social media team, and they know when I call from my mobile number who I am, and that I eat at their restaurants regularly. Never underestimate the value of a good CRM system.

Back to my flight. As we were about to take off, I jokingly tweeted the following:

@petershankman
Peter Shankman ✓

Hey @Mortons - can you meet me at newark airport with a porterhouse when I land in two hours? K, thanks. :)

Let's understand: I was joking. I had absolutely no expectations of anything from that Tweet. It's like how we Tweet "Dear Winter, please stop, love Peter," or something similar.

I shut off my phone and we took off.

Two and a half hours later, we landed at EWR. The fact that a flight got into EWR on time during summer thunderstorm season is a miracle in itself, but that's not important right now.

Walking off the plane, I headed towards the area where the drivers wait, as my assistant Meagan had reserved me a car home.

Looking for my driver, I saw my name, waved to him, and started walking to the door of EWR, like I'd done hundreds of times before.

"Um, Mr. Shankman," he said.

I turned around.

"There's a surprise for you here."

I turned to see that the driver was standing next to someone else, who I just assumed was another driver he was talking to. Then I noticed the "someone else" was in a tuxedo.

And he was carrying a Morton's bag.

Now understand... I'm a born-and-raised New York City kid. It takes a lot to surprise me. A LOT. I see celebrities on the Subway. I see movies being shot outside my apartment, and fake gunfire from any given CSI show, five days a week. I'm immune to surprises.

Except when they're like this.

Alex, from Morton's Hackensack walks up to me, introduces himself, and hands me a bag. He proceeds to tell me that he'd heard I was hungry, and inside is a 24 oz. Porterhouse steak, an order of Colossal Shrimp, a side of potatoes, one of Morton's famous round things of bread, two napkins, and silverware.

He hands me the bag.

I. Was. Floored.

Let's make sure we're clear on a few things here…

1) I was joking in my Tweet. I never, ever expected anything to come of it other than a few giggles.

2) Morton's Hackensack is 23.5 miles away from EWR, according to Google Maps. That meant that in just under three hours, someone at Morton's Corporate had to see my tweet, get authorization to do this stunt, get in touch with Morton's Hackensack, and place the order. Then Morton's Hackensack had to cook the order, get it boxed up, and get a server to get in his car, and drive to Newark Airport (never an easy task, no matter where you're coming from) then, (and this is the part the continues to blow me away,) while all this was happening, track down my flight, where I was landing, and be there when I walked out of security!

Are you taking this all in? Because it happened to me, and I still can't even fathom it.

Think about all the things that could have gone wrong: My flight could have been delayed or diverted. I could have exited out a different location. (Had I taken the AirTrain and not had a driver, I never would have even exited that way!) I could have just missed him all together, I could have landed early, etc., etc…

I have no doubt that countless companies think like that. They think along the lines of "Oh, too many logistics. That'll never work," and they leave it at that.

But what if it does work? What if it happens, and it works perfectly, and it shocks the living hell out of the person they do it to? Like it did tonight?

And what if that person's first thought is to make it public? Like I did tonight?

We live in a world where everyone you meet is a broadcaster. Look around. Think of all your friends, all your colleagues. Do you know anyone anymore who doesn't have a camera in their phone, or anyone who doesn't have a Facebook or Twitter account?

As I say in my book over and over again, customer service is no longer about telling people how great you are. It's about producing amazing moments in time, and letting those moments become the focal point of how amazing you are, told not by you, but by the customer who you thrilled. They tell their friends, and the trust level goes up at a factor of a thousand. Think about it: Who do you trust more? An advertisement, or a friend telling you how awesome something is?

Of course, I immediately tweeted out what happened:

@petershankman
Peter Shankman ✓

Oh. My. God. I don't believe it. @mortons showed up at EWR WITH A PORTERHOUSE! lockerz.com/s/130578715 # OMFG!

And sure enough, Twitter lit up like a bottle rocket.

When I got home, I actually looked inside the bag at what Morton's gave me, and again, was blown away:

And as to be expected, the food was amazing.

Of course, there immediately came a few tweets from the other side of the camp, specifically calling out that I have over 100k Twitter followers, and if I didn't, this never would have happened:

 **@laurahvogel**
Laura Vogel

"@petershankman tweeted @Mortons: meet me at #EWR w/steak & THEY DID" <--What if he didnt have 10K followers? #custserv best w/out glory!

1 hour ago via TweetDeck ☆ Favorite ⊔ Retweet ↩ Reply

But you know what? I don't think that's the case. I don't think it's about my follower numbers. I think it's about Morton's knowing I'm a good customer, who frequents their establishments regularly. If you look at their Twitter stream, Morton's is known for always being on the ball, thanking those who mention they're eating there. Just a recent few tweets from Morton's proves this:

So, I don't think the number of Twitter followers I have played a big (if any) part in this story.

So… What can we learn?

Stay on top of what people are saying about you. Respond accordingly. Perhaps most importantly, have a chain of command in place that actually lets you do these things in real time. Had Morton's had to get permission to make this happen, at 5:10pm on a Wednesday night, there's no way it ever would have.

Complete and utter respect and admiration to Morton's The Steakhouse. This was the amazingly gooey icing on an already great day. Thanks, Morton's.

PS: Possibly the greatest part of the story? NASA the Wonder Cat, (brother of Karma, who passed away a few weeks ago,) got a very unexpected dinner – not of cat food, but of several small bites of a Porterhouse steak from Morton's Hackensack.

Peter's original post can be found at shankman.com/the-greatest-customer-service-story-ever-told-starring-mortons-steakhouse

Creating Your Own
"Wow" Experience

Can you imagine having the kind of impact on your clients that Morton's had on Peter?

We're not suggesting you monitor twitter for notifications from your clients, but it's certainly within your power to establish practices that can provide a "wow" experience.

How about starting with your onboarding process. In the last chapter, we discussed several ways to help ease your clients into a new relationship with you. One way to start doing this is by adding simple little touches to the things you're already doing... like helping them with all those forms they need to complete.

We know of one advisor who sends clients forms with as much information as possible pre-filled by his practice's staff, so there's less for the client to do. They also include a simple, handwritten note saying "Welcome aboard, Mr. & Mrs. Client. We've taken the liberty of getting a head start on these forms for you, so you won't need to spend too much of your valuable time on them."

Another advisor uses her CRM to keep notes about personal interests her clients have shared with her over the course of the sales process. When they come onboard as a new client, she sends them a "welcome" card with a handwritten note and encloses something simple like a newspaper clipping about the topic they mentioned to her. It's a simple gesture that tells the client she's been paying attention to them and cares enough to send something personalized to them.

The whole idea here is to create opportunities that delight your clients in an unexpected way. Walt Disney was a master of this sort of thing. Back in the 1950's, Disney decided he wanted to throw an extravagant Christmas parade at Disneyland. His finance department, seeing that it was expected to cost upwards of $350,000, tried to talk him out of it. After all, they told him, it won't be missed... because nobody's expecting it in the first place.

"That's just the point!" Disney replied "We should do the parade precisely because no one's expecting it. Our goal at Disneyland is to always give the people more than they expect. As long as we keep surprising them, they'll keep coming back. But if they ever stop coming, it'll cost us ten times that much to get them to come back."

Of course, "wow" experiences don't need to be as extravagant as parades. But they do need to be something your clients wouldn't expect or take for granted. Don't confuse a "wow" experience for providing added value. Instead, think of "wow" experiences as added perks of doing business with you. So, if you're considering extending them an extra meeting or sending them a print newsletter to "wow" them, think again. While those are nice gestures, it's unlikely that your clients will consider them unexpected.

When you create "wow" experiences, your clients will be more likely to reciprocate, either by extending their relationship with you, deepening their relationship with you, or advocating for you through referrals... or all of the above!

For example...

Brandon Frederickson used to run a stock picking newsletter and membership program which he grew to over $7 million a year. He noticed that many subscribers would stick around for 6 months and then cancel. So, Brandon looked for with ways to keep them around longer. Initially, he tried sending them a membership certificate (of no real value, apart from extreme psychological value) along with a $10 Starbucks gift card just prior to their renewal date.

His subscribers were paying him $300 per month to subscribe to his program. And his simple $10 gift card typically would eek out another month or two.

Brandon started experimenting with other types of gifts. At one point, he was sending his subscribers steak just before renewal time. In response, he was able to keep subscribers onboard for an additional 6 months. A simple $100 investment in Omaha Steaks brought Brandon an additional $1,800 in revenue.

What's Your "Wow" Culture?

The great sales trainer, Jim Rohn, said "One customer well taken care of could be more valuable than $10,000 worth of advertising."

How can you proactively take care of your clients through your practice's own "wow" culture? It doesn't need to be over-the-top or complex. Just genuine. Here are a few brief ideas to get you thinking:

- Communicate regularly with your clients. Not just an email once a month and a phone message twice a year. Create an outreach program among your entire team to include various forms of communication, including email, phone calls, letters, personal videos, etc.

Make each communication personal and meaningful.

- Host social events. Clients certainly will appreciate being wined and dined. But you don't have to restrict your events to dinners and wine tastings. Maybe host an annual cookout or golf outing. Sponsor a team for community fundraisers and include your clients. Find a common interest among your clients (which is so much easier to do when you work within a specific niche) and build events around it.

- Host educational events. Who ever said that seminars need to be exclusively for prospects? Educating existing clients about additional investment opportunities or services they didn't know you provided can be an excellent way of deepening your relationship with them.

Practical Implementation

Create A Culture Of "Wow"

The first step in "wowing" your clients involves delivering more than what you promised. This may seem simple and obvious, but in the hustle and bustle of daily work, it's often overlooked.

Think about the last time you were completely impressed by a company. You probably did business with them more than once, and maybe even told a few of your friends about it. "Wowing" your clients involves going the extra mile to create a memorable, delightful experience that will create clients for life. Satisfy clients by providing the service or product that your clients pay for in a timely fashion. Then "wow" them by going above and beyond their expectations and provide additional value.

Keep in mind, when clients talk about why they leave advisors, the four most common reasons are:

- The advisor doesn't promptly return phone calls.

- The advisor isn't proactive about contacting the client.

- The advisor doesn't provide good ideas and advice.

- The advisor doesn't return emails in a timely manner.

But simply doing these well things doesn't "wow" your clients!

We'll say it again... effectively performing these basic business activities are simply the price of doing business. Doing these things well does NOT "wow" your client!

With that in mind let's think about what <u>will</u> "wow" your clients:

What are 5 things you can do to "wow" you clients during their first 30 days?

(Send cards, personal phone call, etc.)

1.

2.

3.

4.

5.

What are 5 things you can do to continue to "wow" your clients after their first 30 days?

(Periodic surveys, birthday cards, holiday announcements, etc.)

1.

2.

3.

4.

5.

What can you do to ensure your clients are enjoying the service or products they paid for?

(Follow-up email, survey, client satisfaction tool, etc.)

How can you find out how your clients are feeling? (Surveys, email, phone call, etc.)

When a client isn't happy, what can you do to reach out and make the situation better?

"Wow Your Clients" Brainstorming

Here are some ideas to get you started thinking about ways to wow your clients. Place a checkmark next to the items that you could use to wow your clients. And if this list has sparked a new idea? Add additional thoughts in the space provided.

28 Cost-effective ways to wow your clients:

- ☐ Send a gift card

- ☐ Send a book with a personal note

- ☐ Throw a party for all of your clients at your next major event

- ☐ Celebrate an event, such as a birthday or anniversary

- ☐ Celebrate a milestone, such as number of years as a client

- ☐ Name a star after their company / Family Member

- ☐ Send them a Payday candy bar

- ☐ Provide group/bulk order opportunities

- ☐ Follow them on Twitter

- ☐ Give them bonus items

- ☐ Send personalized address labels

- ☐ Give a night out at the movies

- ☐ Respond to complaints

- ☐ Call them and say thank you

- ☐ Send a handwritten thank you note

- ☐ Feature a client on your website

- ☐ Send cookies, fruit, or flowers

- Donate on behalf of your client

- Plant a tree on behalf of your client

- Meet up with clients in the cities that you are visiting

- Send unique swag, such as a guitar pick, earrings for music lovers, or sippy cups for parents with kids

- Schedule lunch at your office and invite clients to attend and share feedback

- Tell your clients how their feedback was implemented

- Send a laminated reference guide or chart

- Create a video message and send it via email

- Send a small gift

- Pre-order exclusive items

- Send them a travel mug filled with tea

Grow Your Client Value

Business consultant, Jay Abraham, has made a career out of helping his clients dramatically grow their businesses. He has a very simple approach to business growth that is both practical and highly effective. And yet, most advisors will overlook these opportunities and miss out on their rewards.

That's because most advisors grow their practice's based upon an incremental, linear approach. They put nearly 100% of their time and effort into finding more new clients. But, as Abraham has demonstrated time and again, if you grow clients *and* you focus on increasing the size of the transaction *and* you increase the frequency of each client's purchase, you'll increase your revenue and income 100% - 200% or more.

If you work on all three ways to grow a business at the same time, and all you did was improve all three ways by a mere 10%, you benefit from a compounding effect.

Advisors will tell us this approach simply isn't practical because their business is "different." We've got news for you... every business owner thinks, somehow, they are different, and what works in other businesses and industries won't work in theirs. If that's what you're thinking, we ask that you humor us for a moment.

Suspend your disbelief, and imagine a world where, with a tweak or two to your current business model, you too could employ these ideas.

Here's a quick exercise to demonstrate the power of Abraham's ideas. The numbers here are just for demonstration purposes. Let's say you had 1,000 active clients, and you earned $100 per transaction from each of them, and they averaged two transactions a year. That would work out to an annual revenue of $200,000.

1, 000 (no./clients) x $100 (value/client) x 2 (transactions/year) = $200,000 (total revenue)

Now, what would happen if you just increased each of those three categories by a mere 10%? Watch what happens:

1, 100 (no./clients) x $110 (value/client) x 2.2 (transactions/year) = $266,200 (total revenue)

That would bring in an additional $66,200, representing a 33% increase. And imagine if you increased those three categories at the same time by 25%. It would result in almost doubling your entire annual production, bringing your revenue to $390,625.

Where Can You Increase Revenue?

For many businesses, additional revenues are found in four different places:

- Spending less (and saving more)

- Preventing loss (theft, mismanaged business funds, client churn)

- Increasing prices

- Upselling and cross-selling additional products and services.

Any of these approaches can apply to your practice. And since spending less and increasing prices are reasonably self-explanatory, we'll be focusing the balance of this chapter on the other two areas: preventing loss and upselling and cross-selling, all of which are tactics that advisors often, but needlessly, overlook.

The Importance of Preventing Loss

There are three areas, mentioned above, that might fall under this category. The first two, theft and mismanaged business funds, relate mostly to better managing your business operations. For example, making sure employees aren't walking off with reams of copy paper or making un-budgeted purchases of office furniture.

But the bigger, and more critical area of loss prevention is related to client retention. In the last chapter, we discussed the importance of delivering a "wow" experience, which has a direct correlation to your client retention capabilities.

Clients who have a great experience with you and your staff are far less likely to jump ship for another advisor. And a longer client rotation rate means a longer period each client is generating revenue for your practice. In addition, happy clients also offer the best opportunity for free marketing. Not only through referrals (which we'll cover in the next chapter), but through public feedback like online reviews. While you may not be allowed to collect or display testimonials on your website, there's nothing stopping your clients from leaving positive or negative feedback about you on third-party sites like Google or Yelp.

The Importance of Upselling and Cross-Selling

There are several reasons you should consider adding upselling and cross-selling to your practice. Of course, we're not suggesting you abandon your fiduciary responsibility to your client. You must always place their best interest ahead of your bank account. But when you share appropriate complementary buying opportunities (and not just try to sell them more "stuff" for the sake of the additional sale), you'll be in good standing with the ethics police.

If you're not clear on the distinction between up-selling and cross-selling, here's a classic example. McDonald's "Would you like to Supersize that?" is a classic up-sell, while "Would you like fries with that?" is a cross-sell. One is adding to the product or service you have, while the other is offering a completely different, but complementary, product or service.

In the financial industry, cross-selling might mean selling different types of investments to investors, life insurance to retirement planning clients, or annuities as part of a risk-management portfolio. When done effectively, cross-selling can generate significant sales increases for financial advisors.

One common example we see among advisors is when an engagement begins with a single focus, such as retirement account rollovers. In these situations, advisors are likely only supporting one aspect of the client's entire financial concerns.

And, in order for them to provide a more thorough, holistic job in their fiduciary responsibilities, it's critical to have understanding - and management - of the client's full financial package.

Increases Revenue

Obviously, the more your clients spend or invest with you, the more money you'll make. Growth not only comes from customer retention, but also by increasing the overall amount each client contributes to your income. As the Jay Abraham example above shows, it doesn't require a lot from each client to have a considerable impact across your entire practice.

The great untapped market in your practice might just be your current clients. Many of them would be delighted to learn there is more you can do for them to help reach their financial goals. In fact, in a 2015 study of commercial banks conducted by Gallop, only 25.4% of bank customers invested through their banks.

Of those who didn't have more than a checking and savings account, 86% said they would consider using additional bank services that could improve their financial well-being.

Increases Client Loyalty

If you're equating upselling with a greasy car salesman trying to extract extra money from his prey in exchange for items they don't need, let's take a moment to reframe your understanding of the term. The point of upselling is to provide your client with all of their options so they can make an informed decision about their purchase. Upselling gives clients an opportunity to supplement their initial purchase in order to enhance its effect. For example, additional investments, insurance, or financial products might help them reach their goal faster or with less risk. Making them aware of upsell and cross-sell opportunities shows clients that you care and can anticipate their needs.

In fact, studies have shown that client satisfaction is closely related to upselling and cross-selling. For instance, based on the Gallop poll mentioned above, clients develop loyalty for the banks that they feel look out for their financial well-being. Client loyalty can be a problem in the financial services industry: it is common for clients to lack engagement and leave. One study, conducted by PriceMetrix, shows that within the first 60 months of signing a new client, advisors are likely to lose an average of 30% of their client base. Any action that you can take to increase loyalty will help minimize the costs of losing clients.

Increase in Return On Investment

The cost of signing on new client can be costly. In fact, it's been estimated that new client acquisition can run between 10x and 25x the cost of existing client retention. And 5x to 10x the cost of referred clients. Upselling and cross-selling to your clients provides you with the opportunity to realize a higher profit-per-acquisition and receive a better return on your investment. You already did the hard work of marketing, finding, and selling successfully to your client, so why not earn as much from the interaction as possible.

If you neglect upselling and cross-selling, you are leaving money on the table. So, be sure to make your clients aware of the options that are relevant to the goals they are looking to achieve, and, in return, you'll find many of them thanking you for the opportunity to add to their initial purchase.

Increases Client Lifetime Value

When you make it a practice to upsell or cross-sell in your regular routine, you'll find that your overall client lifetime value will increase significantly.

If you're an advisor looking to keep your practice small and manageable with fewer clients, offering additional products or services that are relevant and appropriate to your clients' needs can help you achieve great profits.

And, remember, not only will you increase their lifetime value by increasing the amount you earn form your clients, but you'll also be increasing their loyalty. As a result, you can expect to multiply your additional earnings per client over a longer period of time.

Balances Growth Between New and Existing Clients

According to research, when you increase client retention by as little as 5%, you're able to increase profits anywhere from 25% to as much as 95%. So, while it's great to continue to focus a certain amount of attention on acquiring new clients, it's important to maintain a balance between prospecting and selling to new clients and the ones you are already serving.

A healthy ratio of new to existing clients can help to ensure that your practice is profitable, and not needlessly spending time, energy, and money on constantly finding new clients and replacing those who leave you due to a high churn rate. One way to keep existing clients longer is to provide regular reviews to recalibrate your clients' mix of investments, products, and/or services. This, in essence, is upselling and cross-selling.

Clients who feel that their advisor continues to look after their needs by offering relevant and helpful products and services will be far more likely to stay longer.

Offers Convenience and Flexibility for Clients

In our business, we often find that our clients have hired another agency to provide a service we could have easily and happily provided for them. In those instances, we were at fault, because we didn't make our full scope of services clear to our existing clients.

Many of your clients don't want the extra burden of looking to different providers for their financial needs, when they know they can get everything through you. That's why it's your obligation to inform them about everything you can do on their behalf. By offering them more choices or relevant add-ons, they do not have to take a risk with someone else to get what they need.

Even when they might pay less elsewhere for something you may offer; most clients will choose to obtain it from you. Since you have established trust with the client, you can have the first shot at their business by telling them the related products and services you offer. There are also added benefits you offer, because unlike other service providers or institutions, you have a fuller picture of what your client's needs, goals, and other products and services are. That puts you in a better position to make informed recommendations that others simply cannot compete with.

To a certain extent, you might consider this "one stop shopping" for your clients. Of course, your ability to offer certain products or services will depend entirely on the licenses represented within your practice.

Thanks to the repeal of the 1933 Glass-Steagall Act, you now have more opportunities to represent and offer more to your clients. While not everything on this list may currently apply to your current practice, here are the major sectors in which be able to offer services:

- Cash management and other traditional or non-traditional banking services
- Brokerage and alternative investments
- Various forms of tax preparation and advice
- College and estate planning
- All major forms of insurance coverage, including life, health, and property-casualty lines
- Succession planning of investment, insurance, and other assets
- Mortgage and other loan products
- Comprehensive financial planning
- Accounting and payroll services

As the lines between commercial banks, brokers, and insurance companies continue to blur, this list will likely continue to grow, and consumers will have a broader range of options available to them.

So why not from you?

Something New

With the move toward more and more fee-only advisors, it's easier than ever to add additional services to your practice and charge whatever the market is willing to pay. Some in the financial services world are looking to business models in other industries for ways to grow their client value. One common approach is known as product line extension. You'll often see this in food brands.

For example, Coca-Cola had plenty of success with their original product line. But at some point, they recognized that a segment of consumers wanted a less sugary drink. So, they created Diet Coke. But they didn't stop there. They've also got Cherry Coke, Vanilla Coke, Espresso Coke, and a range of other items under the Coke brand. To a certain extent they are reaching a wider audience by offering more flavors. Of course, some have also argued that line extensions can often cannibalize sales of existing products in favor of new ones.

That said, there's something to be learned from the way line extensions often come to market. And that's by asking their customers. While large corporate brands might do this through consumer focus groups to get feedback on their ideas, there are simpler and less costly ways to find out what your clients want.

Ask them.

Seriously. There's a business model we like called "Sell it, then build it." We've done it ourselves and have seen plenty of other successful variations on this theme from professionals across various industries. It starts by having a client base that has similar needs in common.

As you recognize the same questions regularly coming up or an interest in more education or collaborative investing, for example, you start to develop ideas for additional services, sharing these ideas with your clients, and seeing if there's any interest from them in paying you for the service. If so, you create it... And you've added an additional income stream.

For those who sell information or education, this is a very common practice. For example, David has produced several courses on social media marketing and Facebook advertising. At one point, prior to producing a new course, he emailed his subscriber to float the idea of a course on formatting and design of effective online ads, and to see if there was any interest. At the time, he already had over 13,000 students enrolled in his previous courses, and with more than 100 people responding affirmatively about the new course idea, he went ahead and created it.

So, think about your current practice, your clients, and what common needs they have that might currently be unfulfilled. How can you plug that hole, add additional value to their experience with you, and profit at the same time?

Practical Implementation

Growing Each Client's Value

The second stage in creating an experience that "wows" your clients involves offering more.

Determining what to offer and when to offer it involves a bit of strategy. The easiest way to do this is to determine how you can help your clients today and in the future. The solution doesn't have to be your specific service, nor does it have to result in a sale. Your solution can be as easy as providing tips and resources related to their inquiries. Here are three ways to tactfully increase your revenue while continuing to be helpful:

Cross-sell: clients aren't always aware of the perfect service pairings and may be willing to purchase related items that enhance their experience.

Upsell: Listen to your clients and try to understand their needs. They might be willing to pay extra for special treatment, warranties or monthly programs.

New products: Remember to help your clients by identifying things that will enhance their lives by notifying them of new products or services.

What are your upsell opportunities? What can I offer as a higher level of service?

(expanded services, special treatment, etc.)

What do I do to encourage existing clients to buy new products?

Growing By Reducing Client Churn

Another way to grow your practice is to reduce the number of clients who leave. We use "wow," surprise, and delight to drive more clients to stay longer with you. If you're unclear about churn or how to calculate it, please refer back to our chapter on numbers! The following questions will help identify why clients leave your practice and how to keep them longer:

My current churn rate over the last year is:

What are five reasons clients have left my practice?

1.

2.

3.

4.

5.

Which of these five has created the biggest loss in valuable clients? Why?

How can I proactively address the above reason for clients leaving?

Multiply Your Clients

The best referrals are unsolicited. But, let's face it, those types of referrals are pretty rare.

So, what do most advisors do? They passively "ask" for referrals. Like a line in their email signature file saying, "I'm never too busy for your referrals." Or, maybe if they're a bit more aggressive they'll mention it in a client meeting. "Mr. Client, I really enjoy working with you and would love the opportunity to help others like you. Can you think of anyone who might benefit from my expertise?"

Or how about these classic lines:

"I get paid in two ways..."

"Don't keep me a secret..."

"The greatest compliment you could give me is a referral to your friends and family."

If you've ever asked this question of a client, you've probably gotten a response like "nobody comes to mind immediately, but I'll think about it and make sure to mention you should the topic ever come up."

That's because referrals almost always happen as a part of a conversation. In order for your client to refer you to someone, three things need to occur:

1. They need to be in a conversation with somebody.

2. They need to recognize that the conversation is related in some way to the thing you do or the problem you solve.

3. Your client needs to find a way to introduce you into the conversation.

For example, let's say your client is out to dinner with friends who mention that the husband is due to retire within the next couple of years and they're hoping to find a way to afford a year traveling around the world after he retires.

The moment they mention this, your client will need to notice that the conversation is about retirement planning. And next, if you've done a good job priming your client, they'll need to think about you, and introduce you to the conversation.

Your client's reply might go something like, "Oh, we've been working on some retirement planning ourselves. We've been using Janet Smith. She's great. You should give her a call. Here's her number." Or better yet, "let me call Janet and hook you guys up. She's been helping us plan for our retirement and has been great at showing us ways we can put money away that we didn't even know about."

Of course, the likelihood of conversations like this spontaneously happening with most of your clients is pretty darn low. Why? Simply because it places the burden of responsibility on your client's shoulders to take the initiative to make the referral.

What if you could take greater control of the situation? What if you had a referral system in place to help your clients make introductions more easily and consistently?

Earlier in this book, we discussed two actions you can take to make it much easier for your clients (and strategic partners) to send referrals your way. The first is to focus your business around a niche - either specializing in servicing a super-specific target market or becoming a specialist in a particular service or financial sub-category.

Advisors who have a highly defined niche practice are infinitely easier to refer than "generalist" advisors. Why? Because their clients know exactly who they serve and, in all likelihood, know plenty of other folks exactly like them they could refer.

Consider the difference between the above and an advisor who serves a broad range of clients and has no clearly defined niche. When he says to a client, "I really enjoy working with you, and would love the chance to help other people *just like you*. Do you know anyone who could use my services?" - what does he mean by the phrase "other people just like you?" That could mean just about anything.

But when an advisor specializes in working with higher-education faculty at public universities in Arizona... well, that's another story. Because she has the ability to say to a client, "Are there others in your department who could use my help?" Or, better yet, she could solicit the assistance of her current clients to get in front of their colleagues. The point is, "specialization" has tremendous advantages when you know how to leverage them.

And when you layer a "wow" experience on top of your clearly defined niche focus, you've got a recipe for reveling in referrals.

But neither of these two pieces will be all that effective if you don't give your clients a means by which to refer you. In other word, you need a system. But how do you structure a strategic referral system for your practice?

There's no limit of options. But most effective referral systems have some key elements in common. For example, you can't expect referrals without setting the stage first by making it about *them* before you turn to focus on *you*.

Here's a simple four-step process you can follow. And you can use this regardless of whether you are asking for a referral in person, over the phone, or by sending your client a letter:

1. Make it about them first. Tell your best clients how much you enjoy working with them and point out some of the specific things you're referring to. Are they engaged, do they ask good questions, are they open to hearing "outside-the-box" suggestions from you? This not only makes them feel good to know you like working with them, it also shows that you're paying attention to who they are as individuals. Next, tell them that you realize they probably associate with other people who are similar and who mirror their values and qualities.

2. Tell them that since they obviously know the exact people you prefer working with, you'd like to extend to them the opportunity of referring their valued and trusted acquaintances to you. And be sure to emphasize the value that comes with have them, your important client, be the source of the referral (perhaps, compared to a professional colleague of yours who doesn't have the benefit of being your client).

3. Then help your client create a clear picture of who in their lives could benefit most effectively, and naturally, from your services. Tell them what kind of individual it might be, where they are, what they are probably doing—and why they'd benefit by working with you. Show them what that person

might be dealing with in their life right now (new child, new home, new job, loss of a parent, considering retirement, etc.) so that the picture is vivid.

4. Then extend a totally risk-free, totally obligation-free offer. Willingly offer to host your client and their friend or colleague over coffee or lunch to discuss the work you've done with your current client and learn how you might provide similar assistance to the person they are referring. The idea of organizing an event, as opposed to telling your client to pass along your contact info, puts you in greater control of the process, and limits the amount of "selling" your client needs to do on your behalf.

Try following this process every time you talk to, sell to, write to, or visit with clients for five days straight, and you'll see how responsive people will be, simply because you took the time to ask.

Not All Clients Are Equal

Feedback Marketing Group did a study of consumers about referring their advisors. An unexpectedly high 97% of those polled said they valued their advisor enough to make a referral. But the likelihood of all those clients having the ability to refer effectively (so their advisor actually connected with the referral) is certainly not as high as 97%. So, if you're advisor who prizes the idea of a business built around referrals, you should take serious note of what we're about to tell you...

You must be in full control of your referral process. Don't leave things to chance.

At some point in the past few years, you've probably received an email from a company you've made a purchase from. It might have been a hotel chain or airline. Or maybe it was an online retailer or restaurant. No matter who sent the email, it probably said something like...

How likely would you be to recommend Zipcar to a friend or colleague?

This question is part of a process used to uncover something known as a Net Promoter Score (NPS). Those responding with a 6 or below are *Detractors*, a score of 7 or 8 are called *Passives*, and a 9 or 10 are *Promoters*. In order to calculate your Net Promoter Score after conducting such a survey, you'd subtract the percentage of *Detractors* from the percentage of *Promoters*. So, for example, if 50% of respondents were *Promoters* and 10% were *Detractors*, your practice would have a Net Promoter Score of 40.

While this is a highly valuable tool for addressing and tracking client feedback and loyalty over time, it's also a useful way of identifying which clients would be the best candidates to ask to refer you. In fact, you could emulate the very same format you've seen in your inbox from companies using NPS and send it out to your clients too. And for anyone who responds with a 9 or 10, follow up to ask for a referral.

Now this is simple enough to automate. In fact, we've crafted several email campaigns for advisors using this very process. But can you imagine how much more powerful this would be if it happened manually? Not only could you potentially earn some referrals from your effort, but you could also score extra points for an additional point of contact with your client.

Here's how that scenario might play out: In advance of an annual or semi-annual review with a client, reach out to them personally to propose a slightly different structure to your next meeting. Instead of just covering their financial matter, propose setting aside some time while they are in your office to get some feedback from them. Let them know how much they are valued as a client and that you'd hate to lose them. And that's why you'd like to hear from them about their experience. Let them know you'll have some specific questions you'd love answered, and how important their input is to helping you improve their future experience.

Most clients would be delighted and *honored* that you thought enough to ask.

Once it's time for your meeting with the client, set aside 15-20 minutes to ask your questions. But don't things open-ended here. Don't say "So, how are we doing? Anything in particular we can improve?" Instead, you want to guide them through a series of questions that can help you make specific improvements based on how you conduct business.

Here are a few examples:

"Are we communicating with you frequently enough and about things you'd like to hear about from us? Where can we improve in this area?"

"We do quarterly client appreciation events. I noticed you've been to a few early on, but we haven't seen you this past year. Are there improvements we can make to make them more enjoyable for you? What would get you to come again?"

"What other kinds of events would you find useful for us to put together for clients like you?"

And the one question you should certainly not miss out on asking is...

"When you think back to your initial decision to work with us, there were plenty of other options out there. Why did you decide to trust us with handling your financials?"

Assuming everything you've heard up to this point suggests they'd be good candidates to advocate for your practice, this question, no matter how it's answered, can set up the transition to a referral request. For instance, if they said they picked you because they were referred, you've got a natural opening to explain the importance of referrals and ask for their assistance. If they offer up other specific reasons, repeat back those reasons, connect them to your services, and ask who else they know who might be in a similar situation as they were at the time?

The key to effectively growing a business through referrals is consistently applying your process. Identify the best people to ask. Ask them in a way that makes them feel good about themselves. Maintain as much control as possible by being involved in the referral process as early as possible.

Practical Implementation

Growing Your Revenues With Referrals

Asking for referrals and rewarding clients who refer your business to their friends and networks completes the final stage of the Wow experience.

Effective referral programs are a big win for small businesses because they help clients develop habits that include your company.

When a client is happy, how can I ask for referrals, repeat sales or testimonials?
(Surveys, cards, etc.)

How do I reward clients who refer?
(Surveys, email, phone call, etc.)

What do I do to systematically ask for referrals?

What would it mean to my practice if I could reduce the number of people leaving?

Implementing The Method

"Knowledge is power: You hear it all the time but knowledge is not power. It's only potential power. It only becomes power when we apply it and use it.

Somebody who reads a book and doesn't apply it, they're at no advantage over someone who's illiterate.

None of it works unless YOU work. We have to do our part. If knowing is half the battle, action is the second half of the battle." — **Jim Kwik**

So now you've got the blueprint to the Advisor Inbound Method.

You know how to determine your USP, how to identify your target audience, what's going to attract their attention, and how to sustain their interest until they are ready to move forward. Once you've got them on the hook, you know the importance of dazzling them, and how to leverage those efforts into more sales to your current clients, and referrals from them as well.

You've got the knowledge. But knowledge is nothing without action.

So, you have two choices. First, you can close this book, happy that you've picked up a few new ideas to further build your business, filing them away in a corner of your mind, to implement some rainy day if and when time permits. In other words...

you're not going to do anything. The fact is, most people who invest in "how to" trainings - from books to seminars to online courses - never implement them. Many never even complete those trainings. So, if you're not planning to take action, you're in the company of hundreds of thousands of other advisors happily committed to wasting time, money, and missing out on revenue opportunities because comprehensive, strategic marketing like we've described in the book seems like too much work.

On the other hand, if you're among the small minority of entrepreneurial advisors who are willing to think and work outside the proverbial box to grow your practice, then you'll probably be choosing door number two: implementing what you've learned here.

Throughout this book, we've included questions and action steps to help you form your ideal version of our method for your advisory practice. If you've not yet taken the time to go through those questions, we encourage you to set aside an hour or two in the next few days to give them some serious thought and put pen to paper addressing each and every one. And once you've completed that process, identify action steps you can take over the next 30, 60, and 90 days to introduce the various phases of the Advisor Inbound Method into your business.

Of course, if you're finding the notion of all this exciting, yet overwhelming, we're available to help. Our team at Advisor Inbound specializes in building and automating marketing and client relationship management systems just like the one you've been reading about.

Over the last several years, Ken has been refining an automated marketing process he calls the CORE4MULA, which is a sequence of relationship management campaigns built around email marketing software and strategically scheduled phone touches with prospects and clients.

Here's how the CORE4MULA System works:

1. Our team helps you identify your niche focus and ideal client.

2. Our team then develops a lead magnet offer for you (or utilize, your existing one).

3. Our team builds a customized email campaign, speaking directly to the needs and desires of your ideal client.

4. Our team develops additional marketing assets (as needed) like online ads, landing pages, and even direct mail materials.

5. Finally, our team launches, manages, and optimizes your campaigns.

(…and, of course, we work with you and your *compliance* department to ensure all materials meet the appropriate standards.)

The CORE4MULA System includes the following foundational email marketing and relationship management campaigns:

The Capture Campaign: Capturing leads is the first critical step in any marketing system. (Actually, you need to attract those leads before you can capture them, but that's a discussion for another time.)

The CORE4MULA Capture Campaign makes it easy for your most interested prospects to willingly hand over their contact information without your practice needing to pry it out of them. We'll help you create "no-brainer" offers which speak to your prospects' wants and needs, and thirst for the opportunity to do business with you.

WHY CAPTURE?

Capturing leads who respond to a marketing message that speaks directly to them and their needs provides your business with an ever-growing list of ideal prospects who want to hear from you about your products and services.

Do you build your business through networking?

In addition to capturing leads through advertising and online platforms, we have also developed a networking follow-up system to drive casual in-person contacts into appointments.

The Nurture Campaign: Not all prospects will instantly become a client. That's where the CORE4MULA Nurture Campaign comes into action. Nurturing prospects regularly is an essential part of developing a deep relationship with, and greater trust in you and your practice.

Communicating periodically about your prospects' needs, and how your solution might benefit them, helps you stay "top-of-mind" for that future day when they are ready to work with you.

WHY NURTURE?

Nurturing your prospects regularly (providing valuable and relevant information) builds trust and authority and keeps your practice front-and-center for that day when your prospect is ready to move forward.

The Follow Campaign: As many Advisors have told us, referrals are an essential part of their business growth. But asking for referrals is often an awkward process, and in most cases, lacks any clearly defined process.

The CORE4MULA Follow Campaign is designed to reach out to your existing clients and circle of influence to initially gauge their sentiment around you and your practice.

For those who you have impressed, these campaigns can be designed to request referrals through follow-up emails, prompt you to contact these individuals by phone, or any other appropriate action you wish to take toward soliciting referrals.

If you have an unhappy client, however, this campaign will help you catch negative sentiment before it hurts you, by directing them away from airing complaints publicly, and, instead, addressing concerns directly with your business.

Our Follow Campaign is built around the NPS (Net Promoter Score) principles, the industry benchmark for understanding consumer sentiment.

WHY FOLLOW?

Monitoring and responding to current and past client sentiment provides you an active role in controlling the public conversation about your practice (and putting out potential fires before they become public).

The Clean Campaign: A "dirty" database filled with incorrect and out-of-date information can easily result in mistakes and missed opportunities. The CORE4MULA Clean Campaign periodically engages your network to update their own information and self-volunteer leads and referrals.

Our clients who have run a Clean campaign to their database have uncovered between 10% and 35% of "buyer" leads hiding in plain sight.

WHY CLEAN?

The Clean System identifies golden opportunities to activate "buyers" you didn't know you already had among your existing contacts.

If you are interested in the use of our CORE4MULA system or are interested in exploring our strategy consulting or copywriting services, we'd enjoy the opportunity to chat. You can reach us anytime through our website, advisorinbound.com.

Throughout the pages of this book, we shared a great many concepts that may be new or intimidating to you if you've never considered marketing to be anything more than new leads and referred clients.

Regardless of how you choose to move forward, we sincerely encourage you to take action (with us or on your own). Implementing just a few pieces of what you've learned here can make a huge difference in your practice.

So, with that, we thank you, once again, for investing your time and money in discovering the Advisor Inbound Method. We wish you great success in growing your practice and helping your clients achieve their financial goals.

Thank you for taking the time to read Strategic Advisor Marketing. We are deeply passionate about your success as an advisor. If we can serve you in any way, please feel free to reach out to us via AdvisorInbound.com or to write us **info@advisorinbound.com** or Call us at: 503-300-5999.